LIVING VOLUME ONE:

Praying in the

"YES"

of *God*

ABOUT THE AUTHOR

Rev. Dr. Derry James-Tannariello is Board Certified with the Association of Professional Chaplains, and carries a BA in Religion; BS in Personal Ministries and Psychology; MA in Christian Psychology; Master of Divinity; and Doctor of Ministry specializing in Christian Counseling. She has also been awarded VIP Woman of the Year by the National Association of Professional Women.

Derry founded Chaplain Services at Sierra Nevada Memorial Hospital in California. Hospitals, churches, educational institutions and other community organizations solicit her expertise in training others to minister to the sick and terminally ill, and for help dealing with loss and grief.

Derry is an active chaplain, author, and sought-after speaker known for her compassionate heart, humor and life-changing inspirational stories of faith and wisdom. She is an internationally recognized seminar and workshop presenter and an interdenominational guest speaker and lecturer on topics of How to Have an Effective Prayer Life, Personal Transformation, Relational God, Spirituality and Health and many more spiritually uplifting topics.

Derry also speaks and presents seminars on Spiritual Support in Palliative Care, Bereavement and Grief, End of Life, Ministering to Our Dying Loved Ones, Effective Hospital Visitation and other topics in hospital ministry.

Derry resides in New Hampshire with her husband, where she continues her Chaplaincy work as well as Spiritual Guidance and Pastoral Responsibilities.

Derry is the author of *Heaven Touches Earth: Handbook for Supporting Sick. Terminally Ill and Dying* and *Heaven Touches Earth: Scripture Travel Companion*. To learn more about her other books or to have her as a speaker for your event, workshop, or organization, visit her website: **FreedomInSurrender.net**

LIVING VOLUME ONE:

Praying in the

"YES"

of God

Derry James-Tannariello, DMin BCC

For all the promises of God in Him ARE
yes, and in Him Amen ...
—2 Corinthians 1:20

Freedom in Surrender Publishing

Published by Freedom in Surrender Publishing

For book signings, bulk purchases and inquiries, contact the author at her website: FreedomInSurrender.net.

To order *Praying in the "YES" of God,* or any other titles by this author, visit: FreedomInSurrender.net.

Publisher's Cataloging-in-Publication Data
James-Tannariello, Derry
    Living Vol. 1 : Praying in the "YES" of God / by Derry
        James-Tannariello, DMin BCC.—1st ed.
        p. cm.
    Includes bibliographical references.
    ISBN-13: 978-0-9980152-0-0
    ISBN-10: 0-9980152-0-2
    1. Prayer. 2. Pastoral Theology. 3. Worship. 4. God-Christianity.
    5. Jesus Christ. 6. Holy Spirit. I. James-Tannariello, Derry. II. Title.

Library of Congress Control Number: 2017939654

The author assumes full responsibility for the accuracy and interpretation of the Ellen White quotations cited in this publication, used with permission from the White estate.

Materials cited from *The Positive Way Syllabus* are used with the permission of Robert Lee Law.

Prayers in Appendix C attributed to Winston Ferris are used with permission from Doris Ferris, wife of the late Winston Ferris.

Some of the anecdotal illustrations in this book are true to life and are included with the permission of the persons involved. All other illustrations are composites of real situations, and any resemblance to people living or dead is coincidental.

Printed in the United States of America

Credits:
Cover design by:
Teresa Troy, VCA Design, www.VCADesign.com
Pam Young, Keystone Press, www.KeystonePress.com

Interior design by:
Ray Fusci, rayfusci@momentumtime.com
Ann Cuddy, acc922@comcast.net

Picture credits:
Chapter head backgrounds: © by Dr. Derry James-Tannariello
Callout backgrounds: Bigstock 148224143, 83960315

DEDICATION

This book is dedicated to the Trinity:

To God, my Father, Who cries and rejoices over me.

To my Lord and Savior Jesus Christ, the Love of my life.

To the Holy Spirit, my Inspiration, my Teacher and my Guide.

I also dedicate this book to Bob and Elsie Law, teachers devoted to making a difference for Jesus, dedicated to bringing the truth of God's word in simplicity, to promote the development of personal relationship with our Lord. I thank them for their encouragement and mentoring. Their influence has changed the course of my life, setting my feet on solid ground. A portion of the material presented here comes from their research and development. It is with their love and permission it is included in this book.

I dedicate this book to the members of the Aleknagik Women's Ministry who prayed for and retrieved a computer for me so I could prepare the manuscript for this book.

I dedicate this book to all the passionate readers who have been hungering and thirsting to know God intimately and who long for the assurance God knows who they are, loves them, and has a plan specifically for them.

I also dedicate this book to Kelly Filipps, an incredible woman of God who loved so deeply, everyone referred to her as their best friend. Through her support and encouragement, she was a treasured gift from God to all who knew her. Kelly entered a room and the light of love and joy entered with her. Kelly showed her corner of the world a glimpse of Jesus by living a life entirely surrendered to Him. She lived with a longing to be true to Jesus through her fight against cancer, as she grew to know and depend upon Him more and more. She hungered to understand the power of prayer and how to claim Bible promises more fully.

Her deepest heartfelt aspiration was for harmony and unity within the church. To my beloved sister in God and sister in spirit, though you are no longer with us, may your witness and encouragement continue for generations to come.

"You must learn how to pray properly and that means always praying from the positive side of the curve."
—Freeda Bowers,
Give Me 40 Days for Healing

Contents

"There's a way to do it better—find it. If you need a change and don't look for the better way, the only problem lies in you."
—Thomas A. Edison

PREFACE

INTRODUCING MYSELF TO YOU

HELLO, MY NAME IS Derry Tannariello. I'm a child of the King. That means we're related!

I was given the privilege of raising seven sons. With the credential of MOM after my name, I have spoken around the country sharing my love for Jesus. God was willing to use me without any educational title—until He had other plans for me. My love for the Lord, practical application of lessons learned, and the experience of walking through difficulties where Jesus proved His promises were true, were credentials enough.

All the credentials after my name now might sound a bit impressive, but the reality of it is God put the letters there when they were needed for the job He called me to do. When God calls, He equips.

Like everyone, my life has been filled with much sorrow, heart-ache, shattered dreams, disap-pointments and pain, some as a result of life circumstances, some due to wrong choices or wrong responses. Through all the challenges, there have also been self-awareness, blessings and miracles. I have heard the voice of God, been surrounded with His love, and felt His healing touch.

My desire is to walk alongside you in your journey as I share what I have learned through my stories and experiences.

"Prayer must rise and soar; faith must give prayer the wings to fly and ascend. Prayer must have an audience with God; faith opens the door and the audience is given. Prayer asks; faith lays its hands on the thing asked for."
—E. M. Bounds,
The Power of Prayer

ACKNOWLEDGMENTS

First, I would like to acknowledge God for the many prayers He has answered. I thank God for proving to me I matter to Him. My relationship with Him has encouraged the writing of this book. I want to acknowledge and thank the Holy Spirit for continually urging me and keeping me focused and diligently determined to bring this manuscript to completion. I acknowledge and thank my Lord for all He gave, for all He endured, that I might have the hope and assurance there is more than the disappointments of this life for me; and for all the times He picked me up and held me close to His heart. In return, as I share these teachings punctuated with answers to my own prayers by the application of these lessons, my sincere prayer is that Jesus will be glorified and lives changed now and for eternity. All praise belongs to the Most High God.

I also want to thank those who have walked the journey of life with me; through the good and difficult, the joys and disappointments, and for those who have taken their gift of intercession seriously and continued to cover me in prayer. Thank you to Donna Walsh (my guest from Jamaica in transit), who listened to my thoughts and covered me with prayer, and to Laura Andrews who checked my references, made corrections and offered continual encouragement. My most esteemed gratitude goes to my precious brothers and sisters in Christ; Pastor Dan Prout, Pastor Linda Line, and Robin Duncan who scrutinized this manuscript with a fine-toothed comb, asking questions, offering advice and applauding the inspirations given of God; to Vinnie Ruffo who used her teaching gifts to illuminate the need to "tighten up" the manuscript, and to Marjorie Pryor-Spiller who checked for grammatical errors.

Last, but certainly not least, this book would not be available if it were not for Ann Cuddy and Ray Fusci. They were my constant sounding boards and advisors. It is only by their gifts, talents and dedication that Volumes One and Two have come together.

In this Volume One, Ray's prodding and suggestions pulled out the creativity in me. He devoted endless hours formatting to my approval, and inserting artwork and flourishes.

The value of each person's suggestions and contribution is immeasurable, and I give my love and deepest appreciation to each one.

Derry says:
Embrace life; the joys and the
challenges.

LIFE IS FULL OF UNKNOWNS

Before I formed you in the womb I knew you; before you were born I set you apart;
—Jeremiah 1:5 NIV

THE GRAVEL WAS SLICK as I headed downhill on the curving mountain road. I drove cautiously enjoying the beauty of nature and the strength of the evergreens all around me. From this height the view across the valley was more than inspiring. A sigh of contentment escaped my lips.

Suddenly the car began to swerve. I glanced at the speedometer—under 25 miles an hour. What was happening? The car wasn't responding. I couldn't steer it. What was it I had learned? If the car begins to slide—steer into the slide. I tried. Keep calm.

The edge of the road and the cliff were fast approaching. Again I tried to steer—no response. The edge of the cliff was about a foot away. I cried out, "Jesus, help me!"

I tried the steering wheel—praying. Just as I peered over the edge ahead of me, the car suddenly careened abruptly to the right, flipped over on its side and began to slide along on the driver's side in the ditch across the road from the cliff. There was nothing I could do. (I would later find the steering arm had broken loose from the axle.)

Sliding down the road on my side, I remember thinking, "This is how my son died." I could have been frightened, but I wasn't. In fact I had unbelievable peace. I was at peace because everything was right between God and me, and between my fellow man and me. I was at peace because I had settled in my mind that I want to live or die for Jesus. I was at peace because I know God loves me. He proves it to me every day. I was at peace because I trust His Word and I believe in His promises. I was at peace because I know Jesus wants me to spend eternity with Him.

Think of it, just that fast, one minute everything was okay, the next my life was in danger and I faced death. Life is full of unknowns. One moment things are fine, the next they aren't.

I wrote this book because of my love for God, and my love for people. I wrote this book because I see so much hurt in the world and such hopelessness. My heart aches when even regular churchgoers wonder why they are not able to overcome sin in their life and experience the fullness of God. Some have little testimony of answers to their prayers and the reality of God seems elusive.

I wrote this book to give you the tools to face the unknown with peace and with the confidence that Jesus loves you. He has a special calling for your life no one else can fill. He wants you to be so sure of His love that that love will flow from Him, through you, to others. He loves you so much He wants to assure you He wants you to spend eternity with Him.

My prayer is that this book will be life-changing for you. My prayer is that you will come to know the Father, Son and Holy Spirit as you have not previously known Them— to know Them as your personal and intimate Friends— and to know without a shadow of doubt you matter to

Them, and that the love They are so willing to bestow upon you will fill you up to overflow onto others.

On the following page is a Prayer of Surrender for you, if you have not yet given your heart to Jesus, or have moved away from including Him in your life. It is here if you want to come back to it after this study, and are then ready to have Him be Lord of your life.

PRAYER OF SURRENDER

*M*Y FATHER AND MY GOD, *Jesus my Savior, Holy Spirit my Guide,*

I am amazed at Your love for me. I am overwhelmed with Your interest in my life and Your desire to be such an integral part of it.

Thank You for your unconditional and sacrificial love for me. Thank You that You have a destiny in mind for me which no one else can fulfill.

I choose this day to ask for forgiveness of my sins and accept Jesus' blood covering for them. I am exchanging my filthy rags for His robe of righteousness.

It will be my joy to have You be Lord of my life. I will serve You gladly with wholehearted appreciation for all that You have given, all that You have done, and all that You offer.

Lord, I have not given You my heart before, neither have I made a public confession of my desire to follow You. I ask that You will lead me to a church family where I can continue to grow in You and learn truth. I ask that you will lead me to a minister who will take me under their wing and baptize me.

On this, the _____ day of _____, 20 ___, I choose to surrender my life to You; to offer my heart for Your dwelling place, and to follow wherever You lead me.

_____

Signature

Introduction

Derry says:
It's easy! It's fun! It's rewarding!

Why and How to Use This Book

I can do all things through Christ Who strengthens me.
— Philippians 4:13

GOD KNOWS *YOUR* NAME. Do you believe that? Do you believe there is a God? Do you believe Jesus Christ knows who you are and is interested in your life? Do you believe He is who He says He is, and can do what He says He can do? Do you believe He cares for you personally and is a God of relationship?

Do you pray? Does it sometimes feel like your prayers are hitting the ceiling? Are you angry with God because your prayers seem not to be answered? Have you given up asking God for things for yourself because you don't want to be disappointed again; or are you afraid if God is silent you will begin to question His existence, and then you'll have nothing to put your hope and trust in? Have you wondered why it seems some people have answers to their prayers and unexplainable miracles in their life—and you don't?

Have you questioned if there is any hope or help for your situation? Will you ever have peace of mind? Or have you wondered why you're here? Is there really any such thing as security and joy? Or what love means?

Maybe everything in your life seems secure and dependable, but you wonder how you would face life if it were not. Or is your mind unsettled as to whether or not you are ready to meet your Maker? If the followers of Christ are right, and Jesus is coming soon, do you question whether or not you will be strong and dependent on Him during the upcoming trials, at the end of earth's history? Will you be ready to meet Him face to face?

If you struggle with any of the above questions, this book is a "must-read." There *are* answers to these questions. The key to finding the answer to any of the above questions is in this book. If you really want a one-on-one relationship with God, faithfully put into practice what you learn here. Your life *will* be transformed. I know this is true. He did it for me and He will do it for you. God is no respecter of persons. He loves all His children and has a plan and destiny for each of us. He understands our confusion, disappointment, and reluctance. He longs to have each of His children living in the fullness of His love, care and blessings. He longs for us to communicate with Him—actively praying—sharing and listening.

God's book, the *Bible*, is a book about love; about relationship. Every love relationship goes through a time of learning about each other. Relationships go through a time of growing, understanding and awareness of what contributes to each other's happiness, a time of putting self aside and focusing on each other's desires or needs before their own, and a time of testing.

What you learn from **Praying in the "YES" of God** will not be a formula to insure God will answer your prayers in the way you want. *There is no formula to make God do what you want.* The *Bible* is a book of miracles, not a book of magic. God gives a *recommended procedure* to give you guidelines in praying for those things you need. Just as there is a suggested procedure for communion or for baptism, there is a suggested procedure for participating in "Covenant Prayer," also referred to as "Prayer of Reception," "Prayer of Petition" or "Prayer of Faith." These are all different names for the same type of prayer.

What is covenant praying? That's when God tells us in scripture if we will do certain things, we will receive certain things. He is offering a covenant promise. He does His part, we are asked to do ours—with His help. The procedure is just a suggestion to help you remember to incorporate God's instructions in your prayer life. You don't have to say the words the same way. You don't have to do things in the same order. These are just tools to get you started on the path of building a relationship with the God Who created you and loves you.

The promises of God have conditions. Our part of covenant-keeping is to fulfill the conditions with His help. In claiming (or personalizing) scripture it is important for us to realize God's word gives us guidelines and conditions. God instructs us if we do or do not do certain things, He *will not* hear us, and if we do or do not do other things, He *will* hear and answer our prayers. We must understand what those requirements and restrictions are. This is why I refer to the Prayer of Faith as a divine science. While praying is easy and simple, it, like everything else in the *Bible*, has different levels of understanding and effectiveness in our lives. As we understand the divine science of the Prayer of Faith, we will realize the necessity in obedience and submission, which is life-changing, transforming, and opens the door to a personal relationship with God in a way perhaps we have never previously experienced.

> The promises of God have conditions. Our part of covenant-keeping is to fulfill the conditions with His help.

For instance, I know the minute I call out to God with a repentant heart, asking Him to forgive me—He does. But notice I said God will forgive me *when* I call out with a repentant heart. So you see, even for forgiveness there *is* a condition—a repentant heart. That is what I desire to explain in this book. There are conditions we must meet, with God's help, if we expect the scripture promises to be fulfilled on our behalf.

With all the present world events, I am more convinced than ever Jesus *is* coming soon. May our prayer be to know Him now—here on earth—so we will be ready to meet Him when He does come.

Before you put this book back on the shelf, I hope you'll give it a chance; especially if your prayer life has been disappointing. If you apply it to your life with no success, you can always stop. But if you find the doors of heaven opening for you, you will know you have found the key.

Every part of this book is important and builds one part and chapter on the next.

I invite you to not skip over any chapters. Take the time to focus on each part and chapter in succession.

OPENING PRAYER

The personalized Prayer of Colossians 1:9-14 in the first person for you:

EAR FATHER,

I believe, and am thanking You in advance, that You will fill me with the knowledge of Your will in all wisdom and spiritual understanding as I study this material. Help me have a walk worthy of You unto all pleasing, being fruitful in every good work, that others may see I have been with Jesus. Please increase my knowledge of You and rekindle my passion to allow You to be Lord of my life.

Help me to be strengthened with all might according to Your glorious power, full of patience and longsuffering with joyfulness. Help me to give thanks to You; remembering that You have made us to be partakers of the inheritance of the saints in light; that You delivered us from the powers of darkness, and translated us into the kingdom of Your dear Son.

Thank you that I have redemption through His blood, even the forgiveness of sin that my life may make a difference for the Kingdom.

In Jesus' name,

Amen

"In every promise, He gives us the power to grasp and possess Himself. In every command, He allows us to share His will, His holiness, His perfection. "God's word gives us God Himself."
—Andrew Murray,
With Christ in the School of Prayer

PART ONE

"Whoever knows and trusts God finds
it easy to also trust the promise."
—Andrew Murray,
With Christ in the School of Prayer

Derry says:
Reach for the manifestation of
God's glory!

OUR COVENANT-KEEPING GOD

He who did not spare His own Son, but gave Him up for all of us; how will He not also, along with Him graciously give us all things?

—Romans 8:32 NIV

HAVE YOU EVER BEEN lonely or longed for companionship even when surrounded by your family? I have. If you are familiar with loneliness, I praise God for your longing. You have a depth of understanding about God's pain that others without this experience can never understand.

Our God of love longs for relationship, for communication and sharing, for companionship. He waits and hopes for us to spend time with Him, to include Him in our life, to question His heart's desires for us. He waits expectantly. *And therefore will the Lord wait, that He may be gracious unto you.*[1]

From Genesis through Revelation, the unifying theme is God wanting to have a relationship with His obedient people, who love Him, to live in the place He has chosen, where blessings abound. When His children wandered away and turned their back on Him, He gave them a little space, and then He lovingly reached out to draw them back. When all else failed, He brought correction and dis-

3

cipline to get their full attention. *If you are unfaithful, I will scatter you among the nations, but if you return to me and obey my commands, then even if your exiled people are at the farthest horizon, I will gather them from there and bring them to the place I have chosen as a dwelling for my Name.*[2] *You will live in the land I gave your forefathers; you will be my people and I will be Your God*[3] He wants us to dwell with Him. God has a heart for you and for me, a longing for intimacy with each of us who no one else can fill.

A study of the Holy Scripture shows us close relationships are bound together by **covenants**, binding promises or commitments, with obligation. God says, *They will be my people, and I will be their God. I will give them singleness of heart and action, so that they will always fear (revere) Me for their own good and the good of their children after them. I will make an everlasting **covenant** with them: I will never stop doing good to them, and I will inspire them to fear Me, so that they will never turn away from me. I will rejoice in doing them good and will assuredly plant them in this land with all My heart and soul.*[4] God has never made a promise He would not, or could not, fulfill. But there are some things God expects us to do. He never gives us unnecessary or impossible conditions to meet, or commands to follow. When we do our part as He has outlined (our part of **covenant** obligation), He will do as He has promised. God wants us to put our trust *in* Him, while working *with* Him. We have to do our part. He desires us to surrender to His will, that our victory might be sure.

In Scripture we read over and over of His promptings, of His heart of love pouring out blessings and corrections. *The Lord will establish you as His holy people, as He promised you on oath, if you keep the commands of the Lord your God and walk in His ways.*[5]

He endeavors to prove to us the Ten Commandments, handed down from the glory of Heaven are not restraints to cripple and bind us, but conditions to liberate us and fill our lives with indescribable joy. When we follow His suggestions for living, we find following His way offers a protection against self-inflicted pain. For example the Commandment *Thou shalt not kill.*[6] How much joy would be in our life if we hated so much that we murdered—in our hearts or in actuality? You see, God knows what He is talking about! That law, when obeyed, liberates and allows us joy in our life instead of the bondage that comes when we do not adhere to His way. *You have declared this day that the Lord is your God and that you will walk in His ways, that you will keep His decrees, commands and laws, and that you will obey Him. And the Lord has declared this day that you are His peo-ple, His treasured posses-sion as He promised and that you are to keep all His commands. He has de-clared that He will set you in praise, fame and honor high above all the nations He has made and that you will be a people holy to the Lord your God, as He promised.*[7] He ad-jures us to **covenant** with Him to keep His command-ments. Since every command is a promise, we can then be assured the Ten Commandments can be obeyed through His power. It is a partnership!

Throughout scripture we read that God made **covenants** with His people. He is a promise-keeping God. In order to **covenant** with someone, you need two parties; each fulfill-ing their part of the **covenant** agreement. To my surprise, God initiated a **covenant** promise with me.

When He called me back to college at age 50, I remember studying every spare moment. My priorities were, in order, God first, my family, and then study, study, study. I did nominal duties around the house—certainly nothing extra during this grueling time.

When two of my precious sons showed up on Mother's Day with a parakeet in a cage for me, I was stunned. In my heart my first thought was, "Oh no, of all times—another responsibility—one more thing to take care of."

5

Then I looked at the love and excitement on their faces. I realized how very special this gift was. I hugged them both, thanking them and stating the truth; I said, "I can't believe you did this!"

Several days later my new friend still did not have a name. Believing strongly in the importance of names and their meanings, in desperation I picked up a babyname book and starting with "A" looked at the meanings of the boys names. I was somewhere between the "C's" and "D's" when I heard God say, "Homer." I responded, "Homer? Lord, that is a disgusting name for a bird."

"Really? Look it up," God instructed.

I looked up the meaning. It meant "sacrifice, **covenant**." Then God said, "Your sons sacrificed to get this bird for you. You are sacrificing to obey Me. I **covenant** with you to see you through." Wow!!! Suddenly I liked the name "Homer" and I loved my bird even more. This gift from my sons was their given love and God's **covenant** symbol to me.

He is a **Covenant-keeping God** of partnership and relationship. He wants us to know He is the giver of every good gift. He wants us to know He is responding in answer to our prayers; that He is a personal God Who loves each one of us and desires intimacy. He has put within the *Bible* conditions for effective prayer fulfillment, for us to understand and study. If we, too, want to have that intimacy, and if we are desirous of the "extra" blessings God has in mind for us, we will learn to apply them as God has revealed in scripture. In turn, God will help us fulfill these conditions for answered prayer. This will happen when we learn to come to God with specific requests, praying His word, in faith, for His answer, because He has promised in Deuteronomy 30:14, *But the word is very near you, in your mouth and in your heart, that you may do it.*

Learning to live a life of answered prayer whether your petition is for character growth, healing, material blessings, or physical needs, brings a peace and satisfaction in life not otherwise experienced. Encountering God proves His love and is manifested in the minutest details of our life, even the numbering of every hair on our head. Incomprehensible!!!

"Jesus desired that men look upon God as the Father of mercy, care and love. When they prayed to Him it was their privilege to come to Him as One acquainted with all their needs and to address Him as their Father."
—Edwin R. Thiele,
Knowing God

Derry says:
Personal radiance is magnetic.

An Invitation

I love them that love Me; and those that seek Me early shall find Me.

—Proverbs 8:17 KJV

I'S YOUR MASK IN PLACE? At age six, our challenging little son Georgie, with cherub face and mischievous eyes, was always full of surprises. Today would be another one of those days.

His father, a commercial pilot, was home for the day. I decided to take advantage of his time off to run some errands. In my organized and then controlling way, I called my seven sons together. My parting speech to the children went something like this. "Now boys, while Mommy is in town, why don't you get your rooms cleaned up? You know, *really* clean; sparkling clean! Since I'll be gone most of the day, you can make your bed, clean out your drawers, and check your closet, dust and vacuum. I would be so surprised and happy when I get back home if everything were "sparkling clean."

I kissed them goodbye and left for town. Somehow they were motivated; although I admit I don't understand why. They swallowed my challenge; hook, line and sinker.

Daddy and the boys had a plan. They would work hard for 45 minutes, and then they would check each other's progress. They would have a 15-minute play break together and then they would go back to work.

About midday little Georgie said to Daddy, "Daddy, I don't want you to check my room any more. I want Mommy to check it when she comes home." That was a surprise! Mom was more of a stickler when it came to clean rooms than Dad was.

Daddy said, "Okay, I'll honor that."

When I came home early evening, Georgie met me at the door. He was beaming from one ear to the other. He said, "Mommy, come quick! Come see my room."

I said, "Oh Honey, did you get it all cleaned up?"

He gave me his charming, mischievous smile and answered, "Wait until you see."

As we went down the hall and up the stairs towards his room, I quizzed him, "Georgie, did you get your bed made?"

"Yes, yes, Mommy, I got my bed made."

"Well, did you pick up all your clothes?"

"Yes, yes, I picked up all my clothes."

"Wow, did you clean out your drawers?"

"Oh, Mommy, wait until you see my room!"

"Okay, but tell me, did you clean your closet? Did you vacuum your floor?"

Chuckling now, he said, "Yes, yes, I vacuumed my floor. Oh Mommy, just wait."

We came to his room and with exuberance and laughter he pushed open the door. The very first thing I saw (you couldn't help but notice) was a mess of Christmas glitter all over the floor. I wondered what he had been making. I thought he said he had vacuumed. It looked like he had forgotten to turn the vacuum on. Wanting to be affirming and positive I said, "Honey, your bed looks beautiful!" Look at your room! I don't see any clothes anywhere. May I peek in your drawers?"

"Oh yes. You may peek in my drawers, Mommy." Now he is really laughing.

"Well, your drawers look lovely. May I look in your closet?"

"Sure Mommy, you can look in my closet." He is doubled over with laughter.

What is so funny?" (I thought, *what is the matter with him?)* "Your closet looks beautiful!"

"Honey, everything looks great ... except ... I thought you told me you vacuumed your room. I see glitter all over the floor."

Holding his tummy, he fell to the ground, rolling with laughter. Between gasps for air, he chuckled, "I know Mommy. You said you wanted a *sparkling* clean room."

What a great sense of humor and creativity! Well, it definitely sparkled! Unfortunately, further investigation revealed the glitter was a decoy. For Georgie, it was easier to hide his clothes behind his dresser and between the wall and the bed; instead of taking care of them and putting them away. Things were not as they appeared.

I couldn't help but reflect. Isn't that how we can be sometimes? Don't we attempt to "put on the sparkle" and hide our problems or true feelings?

Do we try to hide those things that are bothering us; those struggles, those questions in our hearts and on our minds? We think no one will see through us, so we come to church or we go out in public with our mask securely in place. In fact, if we are accustomed to wearing it, the older we get, the better it fits. It becomes 'form fitting.' We know the right things to say. We know when to put on the smile even when our hearts are actually hurting.

The reality is none of us truly has "our act together." We all are just at different stages of our Christian walk. We're all in the midst of this battle raging between God and Satan. Since we are still preparing to see our Savior face-to-face, we can expect problems. Let's be real! None of us is exempt. We all need each other. We need to encourage each other. We need to pray for each other. We need to lift each other up. In truth, we're not fooling anyone but ourselves. The *Bible*, in Isaiah 3:9 NKJV says, *The look on their countenance witnesses against them.* **I invite you** to rip off *your* mask and be real.

In this book you will find tools to help you get in touch with and identify the genuine you. You *can*, because Jesus loves you just as you are and He will help you grow and become all you desire to be, and all Jesus desires you to be. Learning to apply the word of God to our life is one of the foundation stones and pivotal points of living in close relationship with God and accepting who God created us to be.

I love them that love Me; and those that seek Me early shall find Me"[8] "Only by love is love awakened."[9] When this understanding motivates us for empowerment, we will be convinced God loves us and we will be ready to surrender completely to His will. We will embark on the most amazing adventure of our life; a life full of stories to share. There will be no need to wear a mask, attempt to put on the sparkle or spread glitter on our bedroom floor. We will be secure in His love. **I invite you** to try to begin seeking Him.

Jeremiah says in chapter 15:16 KJV, *Thy word was unto me the joy and rejoicing of mine heart.* Following that advice, feasting on God's word, will put a *genuine* smile on our faces and exuberance in our hearts.

"Praying in the 'Yes' of God" brings contentment and a willingness to wait upon Him. He sees the long-range plan and answers accordingly. My frequent prayer is, "Father, may Your destiny for me be fulfilled and the enemy's plans thwarted." **I invite you** to pray this prayer.

I remember a time, back when I was a new, new Christian, and I changed jobs. I did it with God's blessing. I had been there for about two and a half months and I hated the job. The job I left was still open. I thought, "I just can't stand this job where you put me now God. I really want out." I struggled and struggled with this thought. Finally with an "I can't do this anymore" attitude, I just said, "God, I can't take this." I went back to the first job. That was a sad mistake. God had a bigger plan for me and I hadn't waited to find out what it was. A week later I found out I was pregnant with our first child. Had I stayed at the job where God had directed me, all my maternity benefits would have been paid. He always knows what is best.

We have a God, a Father Who loves us so much, He is willing to allow us to be uncomfortable for a brief period of time, because He knows the blessings and benefits outweigh the inconveniences and difficulties. He knows what blessing He has in mind. Scripture assures us *God is not a man that He should lie, nor a son of man that He should change His mind.*[10]

We can trust His word. ... *You know with all your heart and soul that not one of all the good promises the Lord your God gave you has failed. Every promise has been fulfilled; not one has failed.*[11]

When God asks us to fulfill a condition in order for our prayers to be answered, we can be sure He will help us. He never asks us to do anything He is not willing to help us do. When God asks, He enables. Every command He gives in scripture is also a promise: a promise of His enabling of fulfillment of that requirement. We need to know what God has said, and then remind Him we are relying on His promises.

In Romans 4:20-24, Paul relates Abraham's faith. Paul says, *He did not waver at the promise of God through unbelief; but was strengthened in faith, giving glory to God; and being fully convinced that what He had promised He was also able to perform. And therefore 'it was accounted to him for righteousness.' Now it was not written for his sake alone that it was imputed to him, but also for us. It shall be imputed to us who believe in Him who raised up Jesus our Lord from the dead.*

I hope you are encouraged to commit to regular study of **Praying in the "YES" of God**. Conditions to answered prayer are what we will be studying together with instruction and stories documenting the lessons presented. Most of the stories shared will be personal. I firmly believe if I am not able to prove by my own life what I am teaching you from God's word is applicable to us today, then there is no reason for you to put it into practice or believe anything I share with you.

I invite you to move forward in your reading with a determination to learn God's holy principles, apply the message, and live life, as you have never experienced it before. God does not want you to have to question His existence or His love for you.

Before you study or apply anything I have presented here, please bow your head and ask for the enlightenment of the Holy Spirit.

On the next page I have a Covenant Agreement for you to pray over and complete. May God richly bless the sincerity of your heart and your desire to walk with Him as your dearest Friend.

COVENANT

F ather God, Lord Jesus, Blessed Holy Spirit; I do now covenant with you, that as I study and am able to determine the scriptural authority of the material presented in this book, I will continue to study and appropriate the instruction given. It is my desire to know Jesus Christ as my personal Friend and Savior.

It is my desire to live a life of answered prayers, walking in Your will, empowered by Your Spirit, and living out Your divine plan intended for me.

Now, with the illumination of the Holy Spirit, I covenant to apply the promises You have given in scripture daily to my worship, appropriating the Prayer of Faith and conditions to answered prayer.

With joy I will share with others what God does for me, with me, and in me.

Signed this _____ day of _____, 20___.

_____

Signature

Derry says:
Faith never stops growing.

Praying the Prayer of Faith

*Now **faith** is the substance of things hoped for, the evidence of things not seen.*
— Hebrews 11:1

THERE WAS AN OLD FARMER who had a horse. He could get to town just fine with his horse. The automobile came along and he had no interest in it because he loved his horse and the horse got him where he wanted to go. But one day his horse was sick and he needed help. Along came a friend in his automobile, and gave the farmer a ride to town to find a vet. After one ride in that automobile, the farmer realized it was a more effective means of transportation.

The intention of this book, as we study together the "**Prayer of Faith**," also known as the "**Prayer of Reception**," is to help you find a more effective means of communicating with God and teach you how to receive answers to your prayers.

Following chapters will teach "conditions" God introduces in scripture as you pray the **Prayer of Faith**. There are certain conditions the Lord expects us to fulfill with His help, if we desire the blessing, or gift, that accompanies His promises. We have no power of ourselves to fulfill the conditions. "Every command is a promise; accepted by the

17

will, received into the soul, it brings with it the life of the Infinite One."[12] We are to present each condition to Him, as a promise for fulfillment, so that the Bible promises/scriptures we are personalizing may be received.

Here is an example to explain what I mean. A close friend of yours knows yesterday you received $500. Today this friend has an emergency. Your friend comes to see you, and says, "I hate to ask you this. I know yesterday you received some money; and I am really desperate. Could you please loan me $100?"

You say, "Oh, I just put that money in the bank. I'll write you a check." So you write the check for $100.

Your friend will go to the bank to cash your check. When he takes the check to the teller, he won't say, "If it is your will, please give me $100."

The teller will say, "If you want this money, you must endorse the check." That is the condition you need to fulfill in order to get this money.

Our Father in Heaven wants us to know He has gifts. He has promises like blank checks that have already been signed in the name of Jesus, with no expiration date. Behind God's checks stand the resources of heaven and His untarnished reputation. You search His Holy Word for the promise/scripture applicable to your need. In order to receive that gift, you need to fulfill the conditions and be "into the position of willingness to receive what God wants."[13] This is obedience to God's instruction.

"There are conditions to the fulfillment of God's promises, and prayer can never take the place of duty ... Those who bring their petitions to God, claiming His promise while they do not comply with the conditions, insult Jehovah."[14] "It should be remembered that the promises and threatenings of God are alike conditional."[15] If we are *not* fulfilling the conditions God outlines for His promise, the promise is not for us. It is for the ones who obey God's stipulations.

As we consider praying for a particular request, we might be less hesitant if we would remember we serve a God of love who has filled the *Bible* with promises to encourage us and give us hope. We serve a Father Who desires to bestow good gifts upon His children. He desires that our joy be full.

Answers to prayer are not dependent upon our feelings; they are based upon the trustworthiness of our Savior. His word is sure. "In the **prayer of faith** there is a divine science."[16] God is anxious to give us insight and instruction regarding this divine science.

We are participating in prayer with our *Bible* open before us. We are following God's direction/conditions in presenting His promises. Then we turn to specific texts that are applicable to our concerns and present them to God for their fulfillment. *Believing* He will do for us according to our best interest, and *Thanking* Him in advance.

This type of worship combines Bible study and prayer. A. W. Tozer tells the story of one old saint who was asked, "Which is the more important: reading God's Word or praying? "To which he replied, "Which is more important to a bird: the right wing or the left?"

If you are unable to find a Bible promise specific to your problem or need, turn to James 1:5 claiming it as a promise, and ask for wisdom from God to find the appropriate scripture. What a change will come into our life as we learn to trust in our heavenly Father, awaiting His response with a heart full of appreciation, as we present His promises for fulfillment.

Watch and pray does not mean to sit still. We are to be vigilant to watch for opportunities to do for ourselves and assist others, as God directs, participating in the fulfillment of our petitions. "You are not able, of yourself, to bring your purposes and desires and inclinations into submission to the will of God; but if you are 'willing to be made willing,' God will accomplish the work for you ..."[17]

Derry says:
Think of presumption as the coun-
terfeit of faith.

Praying in Faith or Presumption

*Keep back thy servant also from **presumptuous** sins; let them not have dominion over me; then shall I be upright, and I shall be innocent from the great transgression.*
— Psalm 19:13

IN CLAIMING GOD'S PROMISES, we must be careful to guard against **presumption**. "**Presumption** is Satan's counterfeit of **faith**."[18]

There are two ways **presumption** can sneak up on us.

1. **Do not leave any conditions unfulfilled**.

"It is **not faith** that claims the favor of Heaven without complying with the conditions on which mercy is to be granted. Genuine **faith** has its foundation in the promises and provisions of the Scriptures. **Faith** claims God's promises, and brings forth fruit in obedience. **Presumption** also claims the promises, but uses them as Satan did, to excuse transgression."[19] If we are walking in **faith**, we will not leave any conditions unfulfilled. Sometimes, especially when we are uninformed, God will answer our prayers anyway. We do, however, have a responsibility to recognize God has ways for us to live a more effective prayer life and develop relationship with Him that contin-

21

ues to grow and increase in closeness. **Faith** is a stimulant for obedience. It is **presumptuous** for us to think God will do for us what we ask without us returning our love and obedience.

Conditions are really commands, and commands are promises. Thus, all conditions are fulfilled in the same way as commands—by treating them as promises. A command of God, a condition of God becomes a promise of victory to the Christian who relies upon God by **faith** in Jesus Christ. When God asks, He enables.

*But they **presumed** to go up ... But the person who does anything **presumptuously**, that one brings reproach on the Lord.*[20]

2. **Do not claim prayer will always be answered in the very way and for the particular thing desired.**

"When we do not receive the very things we ask for, at the time we ask, we are still to believe that the Lord hears and that He will answer our prayers. We are so erring and shortsighted that we sometimes ask for things that would not be a blessing to us, and our heavenly Father in love answers our prayers by giving us that which will be for our highest good—that which we ourselves would desire if with vision divinely enlightened we could see all things as they really are ... But to claim that prayer will always be answered in the very way and for the particular thing that we desire, is **presumption**."[21]

Assignment:

Start a journal this week to use as your "Devotional Journal." Ask God to search your heart and reveal to you:

- if you have been praying **presumptuous** prayers.

- if you have been living a **presumptuous** Christian life.

Journal what God has revealed:

Write out your covenant/commitment to pray with a more surrendered heart according to God's will.

Synopsis of forthcoming lessons:

Going forward, we will be learning the following:

Part Two:

- Discussions on prayer
- Why and How we should pray
- Types of prayer
- Suggested prayers

Part Three:

- Overview of the Conditions for Answered Prayer
- Presentation of each condition
- The application of the condition and its fulfillment.
- Assignment Page (Study and apply one chapter a week.)
- Hindrances: At the end of each chapter you will find a text that is opposite of the condition presented. I refer to these as "Hindrances to Answered Prayer." Please do not pass by this section. Look up each text that is given and see for yourself how emphatic God is about not answering us under certain situations. He is so anxious for us to understand this concept, this "divine science" of prayer, He presents it in the positive as well as the negative so we will be sure to grasp the importance when He specifically says He will answer us.
- Instructions for application of the condition studied. Record your own story.

  Go at your own pace, but as you move forward continue to apply what you have learned and build on it.

Part Four:

- Prayer of Commitment—the "If it is Thy Will" Prayer
- Spiritual Warfare is briefly discussed.

"Successful prayer is not measured by how much we get from God, but how much of Him gets into us and our daily circumstance and relationships."
—Lloyd Ogilvie,
Praying With Power

PART TWO

"… in spite of the fine philosophical positions we may hold or talk, nothing really happens regarding Christian growth until one prays and studies, that is, until one receives Christ."
—Prof. Edwin Zackrison,
Foreword to *The Positive Way Syllabus*, Robert Lee Law

INTRODUCTION TO PRAYER

The end of all things is at hand: therefore be self-controlled
*and sober-minded, for the sake of your **prayers**.*
—1 Peter 4:7 ESV

SOME TIME AGO ON A FLIGHT to a speaking appointment, I sat next to a field representative for a cellular phone company. The technological information he shared with me was amazing. For instance, back then the technology of plugging a cell phone into your laptop and sending work back to the office was beyond my comprehension. Now of course, it's commonplace. But honestly, doesn't it seem like a miracle you can actually have in your possession two pieces of equipment that don't plug into any electrical connection, yet at one end you can type and at the other end, all of those letters have flown through space, and come out exactly as you presented them, hundreds of miles away? Or consider the cell phone—messages bouncing through space, audible voices that are recognizable. It seems almost incomprehensible. But we pick up our cell phones, or turn on our computers and hook up to e-mail with total faith the connection will be made (eventually) and we will either send or receive the information desired. Why then do we doubt God's ability or willingness to send and receive, or hear and answer our **prayers**?

I remember as a child kneeling by the side of my bed and offering my **prayers**. For some reason I had the idea miracles were only reserved for the "missionaries across the sea—that God listened to *their* **prayer** requests." It didn't quite compute that I was of special and significant importance to God as well.

When I was in my early twenties I had separated myself from God for some time. A girlfriend from work had a pastor stop by my home to pay me a visit. I was offended at first. He asked if I would like to have Bible studies. I said, "No. I am acquainted with the doctrines in the *Bible* and with most of the stories." Then he told me he had just started taking a class and was learning the science of **prayer**—expecting answers. He said he had not enjoyed a personal relationship with Jesus until now. I was interested. I invited him in, curious to learn more. I started classes the following week. My life has never been the same. I met Jesus. *I hope if you have not met Him, or if you are not living a life of answered* **prayer***, that your journey and implementation of the following information will change your life as it did mine.*

I found there was far more to **prayer** than I had ever considered. I had been convinced I knew what **prayer** was all about. I found out I understood very little about this gift of communication God has activated for us. I learned **prayer** is certainly *not* to remind God of what He might, without our help, forget or neglect. **Prayer** is not a duty. It is a gift of love. To me, it is the essence of life, the breath of the soul.

Waves of communication that far exceed those of any cell phone are available to us through **prayer**. We never get a busy signal. We don't have to worry about call-waiting. We don't have to wonder if anybody is home. God is always available, waiting, and anxious to share. In fact, often God is the initiator of **prayer**. God calls because He wants to communicate with us. He might have something He needs for us to do or someone to **pray** for or reach out to. Maybe He is anxious to give us some direction to help us avoid a potential problem. Maybe He just wants to insert some ideas for the day's plans or decisions we are facing. In any event, if we have our 'antenna up,' and our hearts are tuned in, we might hear Him call. How will we answer? Answers to **prayer** become a reality when we are obedient and when we take time to communicate. **Prayer** is heart communion or conversation with God as our Father and our Friend. It provides the opportunity to become acquainted with Whom God really is.

Prayer is a special mode of communication that has been provided for our frequent use. At no additional charge we can take advantage of this opportunity anytime, day or night, wherever our location. No special equipment is required. *Effective communication that builds this relationship does, however, have some requirements* that must be met in order for us to make contact or expect to receive a response. These 'requirements' we will study throughout the book.

> One of the greatest privileges given us is the privilege of **prayer** ...

One of the greatest privileges given us is the privilege of **prayer**, the privilege of living in companionship with God. In the Holy Scriptures He has invited us *to come boldly*[22] into His presence. This invitation was given by the sacrifice of Jesus, who covers us with His robe of righteousness, and enables us to come before the Father. *Jesus' name opens the throne room of the universe.*

The great preacher Dwight L. Moody defines **prayer** by quoting a young man who was in the audience when He was preaching. Moody asked, "What is **prayer**?" The answer given, "**Prayer** is an offering up of our desires unto God for things agreeable to His will, in the name of Christ, with confession of our sins and thankful acknowledgment of His mercies."

This pretty well sums it up, but he left out an important point. **Prayer** is also worship—a time to adore and praise God for all He means to us.

The same God Who created the world is anxious to communicate with us ...

Someone once said, "**Prayer** is the moment when heaven and earth kiss each other." The same God Who created the world is anxious to communicate with us, to guide us into His perfect plan for our individual life, to convince us and convict us of His love, and share His presence and blessings with us.

We must be willing to listen, to follow where He leads, to return His love, and to utilize His blessings to bless others. If we desire with all our hearts to know God's heart, we will. God doesn't play 'hide and seek.' **Prayer** is not a duty, and if we look at it thus, we will have no particular desire to know God or His will. God longs for fellowship with us. **Prayer** influences God's actions; it does not change His mind. **Prayer** is not just asking, it is giving, it is listening, it is thinking about what we are saying—not just talking to talk. God responds to an honest heart.

Here *we* are, living in a sin-infested place with satanic attacks at every side, and we **pray** so little. The angels must surely wonder.

Here *we* are, living in a sin-infested place with satanic attacks at every side, and we **pray** so little. The angels must surely wonder.

There are many types of **prayers**. You may be most familiar with **Prayers** of Adoration and Praise, **Prayers** of Thanksgiving, of Repentance and Forgiveness, of Surrender, of Healing, of Commitment (the 'if it is Thy will' **prayer** that will be discussed in a later chapter) and so forth. In this book, however, we are honing in—focusing on the **Prayer** of Reception/**Prayer** of Faith. There is a place for each type of **prayer** during our worship.

With the **Prayer** of Faith we focus mainly on "asking;" but the asking is in accordance to God's will; *Praying in the "YES" of God*. Our desire is to find out what God wants for us and align our petitions accordingly. This form of **prayer** opens our hearts to deep heart searching and sharing. It is not to take the place of the other **prayers**.

That His will becomes our will should be our objective when **praying** the **Prayer** of Faith.

Praying the **Prayer** of Faith is not to take predominance over the more important form of **praying**—Praise, Adoration and Thanksgiving. This is where all of our **praying** should begin, followed by confession from a repentant heart.

When we understand God's promises, and the conditions upon which they will be fulfilled, we will seldom be disappointed. This kind of partnership takes commitment and investment: investment of heart, mind and time.

I remember hearing a pastor share the following example. He said, "Ask someone close to you a favor and maybe 95% of the time they are going to say 'yes.' If 95% of the time they said, 'No,' you wouldn't bother to ask them any more, would you? It is the same way with God. If His answer is always 'no,' why bother to ask Him? We need to **pray** in God's will so the answers are more frequently 'yes.'"

Sometimes we overlook the obvious in God's word. I would like us to look at and study together the "obvious" and if necessary make some adjustments in our worship and **prayer** life according to what we discover. There are things God would have us know that would help our **prayer** life be effective. He wants us to work with Him.

Reading scripture with a scrutinizing eye, watchful of discovering God's instructions will help us actualize the progression of growth that should come as we reach toward relationship with our Lord and Savior. Our findings bring emphasis on God's expectations as well as on His willingness to assist us on our journey.

The *Bible* has over 7000 promises that cover the various challenges life brings. Some of these promises have additional conditions attached to them that solicit God's help and power to understand and to comply with. The condition is obvious in the context of the scripture promise. This is the song I sing over and over in this book—along with "He is able," and He never asks us to do anything He is not willing to help us do. These concepts are the backbone of this teaching.

Many have a resistance to learning the true science of **prayer**. It is to them insulting that someone would dare insinuate they do not know how to **pray**. They are appalled someone would dare mention to them there is actually a method of effective praying being taught that might benefit them. Pride stands in the way of learning the divine science in the **Prayer** of Faith and securing the opportunity of a deeper heavenly rapport.

If only they knew the satisfaction of understanding the rudiments of the science of **prayer** and the joy of experiencing God's answers. "It is a part of God's plan to grant us, in answer to the **Prayer** of Faith, that which He would not bestow did we not thus ask."[23] Corrie ten Boom **prays**, "Trusting in You Lord, brings me into the territory of miracles. Father, it is so good to know that You do not make mistakes when You make Your plans for me."

God says, *Knock and the door shall be opened unto you.*[24] Do we wait for God to open the door or do we turn away in a hurry? When we abide with Jesus, Satan isn't comfortable hanging out around his Victor. Living a victorious Christian life takes more than a rush 'hello' with a shopping list of needs, or a quick 'goodnight' at the end of a busy day.

Just as our cell phones need to be recharged, so do we. Our bonus is when our battery is low, God still picks up our signal. When we realize human wisdom is insufficient and our effectiveness is dependent upon God's rejuvenating power, we will be anxious to ask, "How do we **pray**? Why do we **pray**?" and "What can we **pray** for?

Assignment:

Answer the following questions:

Do you **pray** now?

Are you comfortable with your **prayer** life?

How would you like it to improve?

Are your **prayers** answered 80% of the time or more?

"If the heavens require His guidance, so do men."
—Edwin R. Thiele,
Knowing God

Derry says:
Prayer is the breath of life.

WHY PRAY?

*... men ought always to **pray**, and not to faint;*
—Luke 18:1 KJV

THE KING HAS INVITED US to *come boldly before His throne of grace.*[25] I take that literally, so the moment I open my eyes in the morning, I begin to **pray**. I have learned I can live a victorious life when I know I am safe in the arms of Jesus, led and guided by Him and filled with His Spirit.

Generally speaking, I **pray** before I make plans. I am happiest when I make myself available to God. It is true that sometimes I wonder if I have heard Him correctly. Sometimes He leads me as I reluctantly move forward; but after I have a chance to think things through and submit to His authority, I settle onto a path of adventure and peace. *God never asks us to do anything He's not willing to help us do, so I know when He calls me to do something I can always count on His power to help me do it.*

Prayer brings God's power into everything we do. We make our greatest mistakes when we fail to **pray**. On the other hand, **praying** should be for more than just a quick fix in emergencies, a solution for problems, or for instant healing when we or our loved ones are sick and suffering.

37

We **pray** because we desire to know the heart of God and to understand His will. We claim promises to be one with Him and His purposes. We **pray** because it opens our eyes to the unfailing, unconditional love of God, and because in turn we learn to love Him. It is a foretaste of heaven and plants within us the desire for eternal life.

> **Prayer** brings God's power into everything we do.
>
> We **pray** because we desire to know the heart of God and to understand His will.
>
> We **pray** not to change God's mind, but to know His mind.

*We **pray** not to change God's mind, but to know His mind.* God commands us to **pray**. In our opening text our Savior says, *Men ought always to **pray**, and not to faint.* This is a command that offers us the privilege of knowing God. Many would be surprised if God actually answered their **prayers**. They don't really expect Him to. Mechanical **prayers** don't get much further than 'out of our lips.' It is **prayer** without hope. That is why the study of the divine science in the **Prayer** of Faith is so important. For our Christian growth and personal relationship with God, we need to know He hears us and cares about our future.

God has a plan for each of us to fill, since He created us for a particular purpose. What honor it would bring Him if we would allow Him to fulfill that plan in us. He knows us better than we know ourselves. It is His joy to give us the *desires of our heart.* He delights in our happiness. If we would let Him guide and direct our pathway without resistance, or without first taking things into our own hands and creating problems for Him to resolve, we would experience more *fullness of joy.*[26] "The ultimate object of our **prayers** should be for us to expect God's leading and to allow His will to be done for us, with us, or through us."

When Israel had sinned, *Joshua tore his clothes and fell to the earth on his face before the ark of the Lord until eventide, he and the elders of Israel, and they put dust on their heads.*[27] Joshua had been **praying** from the depths of his heart. He was not expecting the answer God gave him.

God told him to "get up," and He asked him what he was doing. God wanted Joshua to do something. There was sin in the camp. *God was teaching him* **prayer** *is not a substitute for action.*

If our **prayers** seem not to be answered, it is time to go alone with God and do some heart searching. We may think we have done nothing wrong, but if something keeps coming to our mind each time we come to God, we'd better consider it and then take the necessary steps to put the issue to rest. *When we come to God in total surrender with no unresolved issues between us and others, we can be sure our* **prayers** *will be answered.* They may not be answered in exactly the way we would want, but they *will* be answered.

We should **pray** before we study our *Bible.* We should never open our *Bible* without asking for the Holy Spirit to be our teacher and guide. Satan does not want us to believe our Father in heaven is waiting for us with open arms and desires to forgive us, cleanse us, and give us a renewed life. Satan knows the *Bible* even better than we do and is very capable of conducting a Bible study that will slant scripture and lead us from a true knowledge of God and His ways, or cause us to believe God's love and grace will not cover us.

Despite the fact **prayer** *seems like long-distance communication,* we are not reaching out to a God Who is uninterested or too involved to hear us. In Acts 17:27 we are told God is, *not far from us.* We are reaching the ears of our God Who desires that we spend eternity with Him. He will do most anything to have us share His Heavenly home. Jesus sacrificed much for us. God is on our team. He doesn't set us up for failure. He wants us to come out victorious. He's with us to help that happen.

Our Heavenly Father isn't interested in hearing eloquent,
formal **prayers**.

Our Heavenly Father isn't interested in hearing eloquent, formal **prayers**. He is longing to hear intimate and loving sharing from our hearts. Too often He is disappointed. Sadly, many have excuses for not coming to Him; excuses like:

- When I quit sinning.
- I'm not good enough.
- I can't **pray** like so-and-so can **pray**.
- Their **prayers** are so eloquent.
- I don't know how to **pray**.
- I don't know what to say.
- I just don't have time to really **pray**.
- When I **pray** my words don't make it through the ceiling.
- I can't talk to God when I'm in a bad mood; that would be disrespectful.
- I don't think I have really seen any **prayers** answered.
- ...

Soooooo ...

Because we have not recognized our dependence on God or acknowledged our own weaknesses, the excuses roll off our tongue.

"The nobleman wanted to see the fulfillment of his **prayer** before he should believe; but he had to accept the word of Jesus that his request was heard and the blessing granted. This lesson we also have to learn. Not because we see or feel that God hears us are we to believe. **We are to trust in His promises.** When we come to Him in faith ... we should believe that we receive it, and thank Him that we have received it. Then we are to go about our duties, assured that the blessing will be realized when we need it most. **When we have learned to do this, we shall know our prayers are answered.** God will do for us 'exceeding, *abundantly,' 'according to the riches of His glory,'* and *'the working of His mighty power.'"* [28]

There is nothing the devil dreads more than **prayer**; especially intense warfare **prayer**. He loves to keep us busy, involved, unsettled and emotionally off balance. Satan trembles when we **pray**.

Why pray? Because it is our source of strength. **Why pray?** Because we need the blessed assurance He loves us.

Assignment:

Answer the following questions:

In the past, what excuses have you used that have kept you from **praying** or from **praying** for yourself?

Are you willing to make a commitment to study this book in its entirety and work on developing an active **prayer** life?

If you have not already filled it out, maybe you're ready now. Turn to the "Covenant" on page 16 and do so.

Derry asks:
Do you know how to pray or are
you guessing at it?

HOW TO PRAY

*But when you **pray**, go away by yourself, all alone, and*
*shut the door behind you and **pray** to your Father secretly,*
and your Father, Who knows your secrets, will reward you.
*Don't recite the same **prayer** over and over as the heathen*
*do, who think **prayers** are answered only by repeating*
them again and again. Remember, your Father knows ex-
actly what you need even before you ask him!
                              —Matthew 6:6-8 TLB

SEVERAL YEARS AGO at a weekend retreat for women, it
was my joy to lead a young woman to Christ. This
instance stands out as a particularly special event
because I can remember her looking up at me so childlike,
with such searching, pleading eyes, as she said, "I don't
know how to **pray**."

How do we **pray**? While there is a method outlined in
scripture, in the study of the sanctuary model, in the
Lord's **Prayer**, and in Jesus' last **prayer** recorded in John
17, **prayer** in actuality is simply sharing from our heart
inclusive of the components outlined in the references just
mentioned. God longs for us to share the depths of our
heart with Him. Our innermost thoughts, hurts, joys,
wants, and needs, can be opened in complete surrender to
our Lord and Savior Jesus Christ. Beginning with praise
to the Lord for who He is, and ending with a moment of

thanksgiving for what God has done and will do, expands our scope of His characteristics and confirms our faith. I believe God cherishes personal, informal, whole-hearted **prayers** where we express ourselves openly.

To me, **prayer** is more than just **praying** on our knees with our eyes closed. I like to think of **prayer** as fellowship with God. We can **pray** with our eyes open claiming Bible promises and/or journaling. We can actually *pray without ceasing*[29] by lifting our hearts to heaven as we talk, walk, work, play, or turn over in our sleep. Think of it as spontaneous communication from our heart as different experiences manifest throughout the day. Mind you, I am not talking about mindless chatter, or "vain repetitions" that would be a waste of God's time. I'm referring to being much in **prayer**, continually in **prayer**, and **praying** without ceasing to keep our mind on heavenly things and protect ourselves from being overcome by the world's allurements.

I recently learned James, the brother of Jesus, who at first did not believe in Jesus, was later referred to as "camel knees." His knees became worn and misshapen from spending so much time on them in communion with the Lord. James was a passionate "**pray-er.**"

Kneeling is not the only posture for **praying**, yet it is the most honoring. It shows our reverence and submission for our King of Kings, and Lord of Lords.

What posture do we assume? Do we kneel, stand, sit, or lie? The *Bible* gives us the answer as we study the examples given. Jesus **prayed** alone, kneeling in the Garden of Gethsemane,[30] but He was standing at Lazarus tomb, with His eyes open, lifted toward heaven.[31] Moses prostrated himself before the Lord forty days and forty nights in intercession[32] as did King David pleading for the life of his son.[33] David also **prayed** from his bed.[34]

How often did they **pray**? David **prayed** faithfully seven times a day praising God for His righteousness.[35] Daniel, who was the chief governor over the whole realm of Medes and Persians, **prayed** three appointed times a day without fail, even under threat of death. Although this man of high authority was pressed with responsibility, he did not neglect his appointments—set time—with God. Could it be this is the secret of his wise leadership and the recognition of honor recorded in scripture?

God invites us to "*come boldly*"[36] before His throne of grace. That invitation should remove all fear. We have been invited by our loving Father who is anxious for us to spend time with Him. And what would you think He wants us to do in His presence? Visit. He wants us to talk to Him, while He listens, and He wants to talk to us while we listen—two-way communications.

How do you talk to your friends? Do you do all the talking and not let them get a word in? Do you repeat yourself frequently, boring them to death? Do you continually repeat their name reminding them you know whom they are? Do you end your dissertation abruptly and cut them off not even giving them a chance to respond? How do you talk to your friends? We are to talk to God the same way, as our friend.

God instructs us, *When you **pray**, use not vain repetitions, as the heathen do: for they think that they shall be heard for their much speaking. Be not therefore like them: for your Father knows what things you have need of, before you ask Him.*[37] Show respect. Don't continually repeat His Name.

I wonder how God feels when day after day we barge into His presence, pour forth our petitions, say "Amen," and cut Him off? How irreverent is that? Do we really realize Whom it is we are approaching? Is there really no time for or thought of respect, honor, praise and adoration? Do we wonder about God's feelings?

If our rush appointment with God is in the morning, do we take time to offer Him a greeting of adoration? Do we question how He has spent the night? He probably witnessed some pretty horrendous scenes, some very heart-wrenching episodes.

Maybe before we storm into God's presence and drop our load of wants and needs, we might just take a minute or two and bask in His awesome presence, and experience His love and warmth, meditate on His glory, and listen for His response. God looks forward to our time together even if we don't feel we really know how to **pray**. He just wants us to be real with Him. Whenever we turn our thoughts to God, He is there. When we express ourselves from the heart, God will correct our thinking and help us grow. We can learn the most when we are honest.

God is able to deal with any emotion we have when we come to Him. There are stories in the *Bible* where God is called upon in anger, in frustration, in despair, in protest, in arrogance, and with accusations, as well as with positive acclamations. God listens to us all. No matter how we feel, we can come. So why are we reticent to come before our Father?

Perhaps it would be easier to understand His willingness if we have had a positive relationship with our earthly parents. It is hard for me to imagine a child coming to his daddy pouring out his heart and have his daddy just stand there, not speaking, not hugging or responding in any way. And yet, I have heard stories of worse. But our heavenly Father is more anxious to commune with us than the most perfect earthly father. God wants us to be comfortable in His presence. He doesn't stand back uninterested.

If we come into God's presence as anxious to hear from Him as we are to talk to Him, our minds won't wander. If they do, we can ask the Holy Spirit to take our mind captive. As our love for Him continues to grow so will our desire to spend time with Him.

How do we **pray**? By following the pattern of the Lord's **Prayer**, we should begin with adoration, include time for confession and repentance, a time of thanking God, a time of requesting for others (intercession) and ourselves, and then end by asking in the name of Jesus.[38] Jesus' name opens the door of heaven for us and gives our **prayers** efficacy. *For **through Him** we have access in one Spirit unto the Father.*[39]

How do we pray? The Bible is full of the promises of God. He is waiting for us to present these promises to Him for fulfillment. God's promises give us unlimited prayer material.

There is little time left before our King returns. Strong communication with our Father will prepare us for the days soon coming. His instructions are clear and He states *by His promises* we will *participate in the divine nature and escape the corruption in the world caused by evil desires.*[40]

But if from there you seek the Lord your God, you will find Him if you look for Him with all your heart and with all your soul.—Deuteronomy 4:29 NIV.

By following the pattern of the Lord's Prayer, what components are mentioned above that we should include in our prayers?

1.

2.

3.

4.

5.

Assignment:

Answer the following questions:

What have you learned about prayer in this chapter?

What changes do you need to incorporate into your prayer life?

HOW GOD ANSWERS PRAYER

*He shall call upon me, and I will **answer** him: I will be with him in trouble; I will deliver him, and honor him.*
—Psalm 91:15

The blessing of the Lord makes one rich, and He adds no sorrow with it.
—Proverbs 10:22

THIS IS ONLY MEANT TO BE a brief overview of how God **answers** prayer. God reveals Himself and His will in many ways; through His word, through providential workings, through friends and relatives, through the circumstances of everyday living, through nature, through that still small voice or pictures in our minds, dreams or visions. As we become more familiar with the voice of our Good Shepherd we will follow His lead more quickly. As we recognize what God reveals to us, we have a choice as to how we are going to respond.

God honors the sincere heart, the obedient heart. Many times I have asked God to affirm that when I think it is Him speaking, it *really* is. He wants us to recognize His voice. He honors our desire to know and understand His directions. He does not want us to take a misstep. If we fail to hear Him correctly, we can be assured He will intervene and set us back on track. Throughout this book, I will share a variety of ways God has **answered** my prayers. God will enable us to fulfill His will if we keep in communion with Him. Each of us was born to fill a particular place in God's Kingdom plans. I pray for His destiny for us to be fulfilled.

We can know the will of God by His promises. If you do not know the thing you are praying for is according to God's will, then you must say, "if it is Thy will." But if you know God has promised it, and if you have filled the conditions, you know the gift is yours. If there is not a particular promise for a given situation can we still know the will of God? In many cases we can. *It is the work of the Holy Spirit to reveal God's will to us.*[41]

When we are praying God's heart, and sure of the intention of the scripture promise we are claiming, then: "When our prayers seem not to be **answered**, we are to cling to the promise; for the time of **answering** will surely come, and we shall receive the blessing when we need it most ... God is too wise to err, and too good to withhold any good thing from them that walk uprightly. Then do not fear to trust Him, even though you do not see the immediate **answer** to your prayers. Rely upon His sure promise, 'Ask, and it shall be given you.'"[42]

God does nothing halfway. He is a God of plenty Who gives you the best for you.

Assignment:

How has God spoken to you? (If you have never heard God speak, you may look forward to this new experience as you study and learn.)

What prayers has God specifically **answered** in your life? Record them here. Some of you may need additional paper! (If you are not aware of any prayers being **answered**, please do not be discouraged. Keep reading this book in anticipation of the stories you will be able to record one day soon.)

"When Jesus was upon the earth, he taught his disciples how to pray. He directed them to present their daily needs before God, and to cast all their care upon Him. And the assurance he gave them that their petitions should be heard, is assurance also to us."
—Ellen G. White,
Steps to Christ

Derry says:
Jesus only has to do something
once to be our example.

CHRIST AS OUR EXAMPLE

And there came a voice from the cloud saying, This is My
beloved Son: hear Him.
—Luke 9:35 KJV

A S I HAVE FOCUSED more and more on Jesus, I am learning by His **example** how to conduct my life. As I study, I realize Jesus only had to do something once in order to be an **example** to me. He is our ultimate role model.

Our Savior **exemplifies** the absolute necessity of prayer. As we examine His prayer life we will increase our understanding of the components of prayer and the necessity of an ongoing commune with God, in Jesus' name. So important to Him was prayer, often He would go without food or sleep in order to spend time conversing with His Father. He knew the effectiveness of His work depended upon receiving instruction for the day, and the guidance of the Spirit.

No matter how busy our Lord was, He always took time to pray. Multitudes would follow and wait while Jesus took time to be alone to listen to His Father. *But Jesus Himself would often slip away to the wilderness and pray.*[43] Jesus prayed and preached quoting from Old Testament scriptures. We, like Jesus, are to *Seek first the Kingdom of God and His righteousness.*[44]

Scripture tells us how Jesus spent the day healing the sick and casting out devils.[45] In the morning while others were still sleeping, Jesus got up, went to a place where He could be alone, and prayed. Jesus went boldly before the throne of grace, to His Father, for direction, for energy to go on, for power, for victory over sin, and to fill up His love cup so He could keep giving. He came "forth invigorated and refreshed, braced for duty and trial."[46]

In the book of Luke[47], we are told Jesus also prayed all night. The next morning, after having consulted with His Father, He called together His disciples and picked twelve apostles. Have you ever spent the night in prayer when facing major decisions?

I have seldom prayed *all* night; but there have been many nights I have prayed when I turned over in bed. At times I feel my strength has been used up. In the morning I come to God for energy and wisdom to complete the tasks ahead.

Jesus went up into the mountains to pray, sometimes alone,[48] and sometimes with friends. One time when Peter, James and John were with Him, they heard a voice from Heaven say, *This is My beloved Son, hear Him.*[49]

Jesus knew He was dependent on the Father. They communed together often. The power of prayer, showing God's response, is recorded for us at Jesus' baptism. The heavens opened and the Holy Spirit in the form of a dove appeared and rested upon Him. I wish I had been there. That must have been awesome—to hear God's voice and see the dove rest on Jesus!

Jesus gave His disciples counsel on spiritual warfare and fasting too. They wondered why they could not cast out the evil spirit. Jesus answered, *This kind can come out by nothing save by prayer and fasting.*[50] Why was fasting necessary? Can God not hear us unless we afflict ourselves and go without food?

A true fast calls for complete consecration and surrender. I believe there are certain times God wants us to show Him we are in earnest; that what we are asking for matters so much to us, we would actually be willing to sacrifice the comfort of our bellies in order to hear God's voice or invite His interventions. God wants us to realize we are absolutely dependent on Him. Will we trust Him? Is our faith grounded in Jesus? When we study "fasting" in scripture we see it is not an option. Jesus instructs us, encourages us, and exemplifies to us the need and importance of making fasting a regular part of our worship and prayer life.

When the disciples asked, "Lord, teach us to pray," they spoke for us as well. Throughout the ages this request has been echoed. To question, to understand what we can do or how we can come to the Father with the knowledge that our hearts have been heard—expectant of His response—is the deepest heart cry of every sincere Christian.

The Lord answered them by giving them what we refer to as the 'Lord's Prayer.' As we reflect on the Lord's Prayer, [51] we notice Jesus sandwiched His prayer with praise. While we are, of course, not restricted to these words alone, we need to realize we are being taught to come to God with praise, thanksgiving, confession, petitions, and to claim His provisions, mercy and forgiveness as He has promised. We should daily offer this prayer our Lord taught His disciples to pray, and then live in the confidence of that prayer. Its principles are foundational to sound understanding and will open our minds in surrender to God's will.

Jesus left us another **example** of prayer in John 17. Prior to Jesus leaving this earth He went before our Father and interceded for His disciples and for us, as future believers. His request for us, as He commissioned us into all the world, was that we would be one with Him and the Father, that our joy would be full, for our protection from Satan's power, and that we would be pure and holy as we learn the words of truth. Jesus prayed for unity; unity in love as He is with His Father. The requests made in this prayer should be often repeated from our lips.

Most of us will remember the prayer in the Garden of Gethsemane where Jesus agonized with His Father, begging Him for a way to avoid the cross. He pleaded for God to intervene if there were any other way sinners could be saved. Nevertheless, He was willing to go through with it. His Father watched and listened intently. I would not be surprised if He did so with a broken heart and tears streaming down His face as He denied Jesus' petition. Jesus' defeat or victory would affect all humanity. With humility Jesus surrendered and submitted. That last sentence is our cue. We should bring our petitions before God with self-abandonment, in total surrender and submission.

Before Jesus left His friends, He gave them the assurance He would not leave them to fend for themselves. He would send them a Comforter, the Holy Spirit, as a Helper. To receive, we must follow Jesus' **example**. We need to take time to be alone with God, our Father, and wait for Him to fill us and anoint us for His service every day. When we know we are walking in God's appointed plan for our life, that we are where He has destined for us to be, then we will have a confidence and firmness, courage and determination that no problem, heartache or crisis can thwart.

To be a Christian is to be Christ-like. To become Christ-like is the only thing in the world worth caring about. It should be our one priority. Instead of pleasing ourselves or pushing to have our own way, we must seek to reflect Him. That means when we spend time in prayer focusing on Him, we will come to know Him. We will relinquish our sins, inviting Him to transform us, to make His will our will with a desire to do His work.

> We are forming characters for heaven. No character can be complete without trial and suffering. We must be tested. We must be tried. Christ bore the test of character in our behalf that we might bear this test in our own behalf through the divine strength He has brought to us. Christ is our **example** in patience, in forbearance, in meekness and lowliness of mind. He was at variance and at war with the whole ungodly world, yet He did not give way to passion and violence manifested in words and actions, although receiving shameful abuse in return for good works. He was afflicted, He was rejected and despitefully treated, yet He retaliated not. He possessed self-control, dignity, and majesty. He suffered with calmness and for abuse gave only compassion, pity, and love.

> Imitate your Redeemer in these things. Do not get excited when things go wrong. Do not let self arise and lose your self-control because you fancy things are not as they should be. Because others are wrong is no excuse for you to do wrong. Two wrongs will not make one right. You have victories to gain in order to overcome as Christ overcame.

> Christ never murmured, never uttered discontent, displeasure, or resentment. He was never disheartened, discouraged, ruffled nor fretted. He was patient, calm, and self-possessed under the most exciting and trying circumstances. All His works were performed with a quiet dignity and ease, whatever commotion was around Him. Applause did not elate Him. He feared not the threats of His enemies. He moved amid the world of excitement, of violence and crime, as the sun moves above the clouds. Human passions and commotions and trials were beneath Him. He sailed like the sun above them all. Yet He was not

indifferent to the woes of men. His heart was ever touched with the sufferings and necessities of His brethren, as though He himself was the one afflicted. He had a calm inward joy, a peace which was serene. His will was ever swallowed up in the will of His Father. Not My will but Thine be done, was heard from His pale and quivering lips.[52]

For all the promises of God find their Yes in Him. That is why it is through him that we utter our Amen to God for His glory.[53]

"Follow the Savior's **example**, and let your time alone with God, in prayer, set the agenda for your life."[54]

Assignment:

Answer the following questions:

In what ways do you need to be more like Jesus?

How will the **example** of Jesus' prayer life motivate you in your prayer life?

What components in Jesus' prayers, did you find you were not including in your own daily prayers?

"The imperative question is: Do you want to possess the Holy Spirit, or do you want the Holy Spirit to possess you? Are you willing to respond in heartfelt obedience?"
—Derry James-Tannariello

Derry says:
Don't be afraid—be expectant.

PRAYER FOR THE HOLY SPIRIT

*If ye then, being evil, know how to give good gifts unto your children; how much more shall your heavenly Father give the **Holy Spirit** to them that ask Him?*
—Luke 11:13 KJV

ABOUT 15 YEARS AGO several of us longed for a special touch from Jesus. We longed for the deepest sense of the **Holy Spirit's** presence in our life. We studied and prayed. Then we decided we would fast and pray for three days. At the end of the three days we went before God and fervently prayed for the outpouring, anointing, and baptism of the **Holy Spirit**.

Have you ever prayed for the occupancy or involvement of the **Holy Spirit** in your life? I can remember for the first few years of my new Christian walk, I was actually afraid to pray for the "baptism" of the **Holy Spirit**. (Now if you are a Pentecostal, you probably have no understanding of how anyone could be resistant or fearful of praying for the **Holy Spirit**. But trust me, if you weren't raised Pentecostal, the **Holy Spirit** doesn't get due attention.) Anyway, I prayed the promise in Luke 11:13 for the gift of the **Holy Spirit**, but in my mind I think I was only asking for a little bit; you know, enough to make it through the day with a pleasant disposition. To think of really being filled with, and used by, the **Holy Spirit** was another story. I was worried about what God might ask of me, or have me do for Him. Have any of you ever felt that way? I hope not. But if you have, I want to put your mind at rest.

There are no additional conditions to be fulfilled when requesting the presence of the **Holy Spirit** *except* to ask with a true desire to receive. God is anxious to share the gift of the **Holy Spirit** with us as indicated in our opening text. Just ask! If we are not moving under the guidance of the **Holy Spirit**, we need to come before God and ask Him to renovate our heart and mind that we might come into oneness with Christ Jesus through the assistance of the **Holy Spirit**, our Comforter, our Teacher and our Guide.[55]

"Through the **Spirit** God works in His people *'to will and to do of His good pleasure.'*" [56]

It is interesting to look at what became of our little group; those who participated wholeheartedly in that day of fasting and prayer. Our lives reveal the evidence that our gifts and talents were multiplied and our wisdom and knowledge accentuated. "Hearts that respond to the influence of the **Holy Spirit** are the channels through which God's blessing flows."[57] "Human agencies are the hands of heavenly instrumentalities ..."[58]

How sad it is we waited so long for God to have His way with us and for us to embrace His most precious gift, given on behalf of Jesus. It is the work of the **Holy Spirit** to introduce us to God and make God real to us when we pray and to intercede for us as we pray. *Likewise the* **Spirit** *helps us in our weakness. For we know not what to pray for as we ought, but the* **Spirit** *Himself intercedes for us with groaning too deep for words. And He who searches hearts knows what is the mind of the* **Spirit**, *because the* **Spirit** *intercedes for the saints according to the will of God.*[59] We need to remember our own inability to pray as we should and depend upon His intercessions on our behalf and request the **Holy Spirit** to guide us, and speak through us as we pray. To pray in the **Spirit**, we must surrender our will to God. I pray the **Holy Spirit** will take my mind captive as I pray and worship so my mind doesn't wander and so Satan can't storm my thoughts. Our prayer should be for a daily, continual infilling of the **Holy Spirit**, that God might be glorified through us in all ways. As things come to our mind to present in prayer, it is the **Holy Spirit** Who is alerting us of important issues that need to come before the throne of God.

When we are filled with the **Holy Spirit** we cannot help but affect others around us. Those who are open to God will be drawn; those who are against God will be repelled. We are to be channels of the **Holy Spirit** in turning people to the true source of happiness. How do we do that? First we must learn the lesson of self-distrust and allow the **Holy Spirit** to direct us. "The most childlike disciple is the most efficient in labor for God."[60]

> When we are filled with the **Holy Spirit** we cannot help but affect others around us.

*I will send Him (the **Holy Spirit**), to you. And when He comes He will convince the world of sin and of righteousness and of judgment: ...He will guide you into all the truth ...[61] But the Counselor, the **Holy Spirit**, whom the Father will send in My name, He will teach you all things, and bring to your remembrance all that I have said to you.[62]*

If we are of one heart and mind with the **Holy Spirit** as we are admonished to be in scripture,[63] uniting our weakness to His strength, we can live a consistent life of a true, pure Christian. It is our responsibility to make people feel comfortable; and let the **Holy Spirit** make them feel uncomfortable.

We need to have the praise of God in our hearts and voice so there is no opportunity to grieve the **Holy Spirit** by division, dissensions, fault-finding, incriminations, and pride. We must be pure in heart desiring all for our Lord.

"To have the religion of Christ means that you have absolutely surrendered your all to God, and consented to the guidance of the **Holy Spirit**. Through the gift of the **Holy Spirit** moral power will be given you, and not only will you have your former entrusted talents for the service of God, but their efficiency will be greatly multiplied. The surrender of all our powers to God greatly simplifies the problem of life. It weakens and cuts short a thousand struggles with the passions of the natural heart."[64] As we are open to the influence of the **Holy Spirit** we will also receive strength to overcome.

> We cannot use the **Holy Spirit**. The **Spirit** is to use us ...

"Christ has promised the gift of the **Holy Spirit** to His church, and the promise belongs to us as much as to the first disciples. But like every other promise, it is given on conditions. There are many who believe and profess to claim the Lord's promise; they talk *about* Christ and *about* the **Holy Spirit**, yet receive no benefit. They do not surrender the soul to be guided and controlled by the divine agencies. *We cannot use the **Holy Spirit**. The **Spirit** is to use us ...* but many will not submit to this. They want to manage themselves. This is why they do not receive the heavenly gift. Only to those who wait humbly upon God, who watch for His guidance and grace, is the Spirit given. The power of God awaits their demand and reception. This promised blessing, claimed by faith, brings all other blessings in its train. It is given according to the riches of the grace of Christ, and He is ready to supply every soul according to the capacity to receive."[65]

The **Holy Spirit** is always striving with us. If we are open to listen and obey, transformation can take place and relationship with Christ strengthened with unreserved consecration. "Those who are in connection with God are channels for the power of the **Holy Spirit**. The inner life of the soul will reveal itself in the outward conduct."[66] "A driving dissatisfaction with ourselves, our relationship with God, and the world in which we live is evidence that we are in touch with the **Holy Spirit**."[67]

"To Jesus, Who, (in His humanity) emptied Himself for the salvation of lost humanity, the **Holy Spirit** was given without measure. So it will be given to every follower of Christ when the whole heart is surrendered for His indwelling. Our Lord Himself has given the command, 'Be filled with the Spirit'[68] and this command is also a promise of its fulfillment."[69]

The promise requesting the **Holy Spirit** is waiting within the blessed pages of scripture. The **Holy Spirit** is anxiously waiting in love, to be invited to be part of your life. May you experience the fullness of joy as you embrace the **Holy Spirit** and the gifts He is desirous of imparting to you for the furtherance of the Kingdom.

Jesus says, *And I will pray the Father and He shall give you another Comforter, that He may abide with you forever.*[70]

Assignment:

Have you ever prayed for the baptism of the **Holy Spirit**? If not, why do you think that is?

Do you want to receive the gift of the **Holy Spirit**? If not, why do you think that is?

What gifts would you desire for the **Holy Spirit** to impart to you?

Would God add anything to that list? What?

Research what names or symbols are given to, or associated with, the **Holy Spirit** in scripture, and write those in your journal

"Prayer is designed to adjust you to God's
will, not to adjust God to your will."
—Henry T. Blackaby,
Experiencing God Day by Day

OPEN THE DOORS OF HEAVEN WITH
PRAISE, ADORATION AND THANKSGIVING

By Him therefore let us offer the sacrifice of praise to God continually, that is the fruit of our lips giving thanks to His name.

—Hebrews 13:15 KJV

THE YEAR I RETURNED TO SCHOOL to complete my degree was a very busy one. There were times the load seemed pretty heavy and I felt a bit overwhelmed. As I sat struggling at my computer attempting to meet deadlines, I realized without my Father's help all my attempts to succeed would be futile. In these pressured moments I found relief in soothing, praise-filled, background music. The music filled my heart with thoughts of love and thanksgiving to my heavenly Father, and brought composure and peace to my being.

This awareness emphasized the point I believe God is attempting to get through to us: **Praise** is more for us, but it ministers to God's Heart too! *By Him therefore, let us offer the sacrifice of **praise** to God continually, that is the fruit of our lips, giving **thanks** to His name.*[71]

If life seems filled with unanswered questions that are crowding us, and we find ourselves over our heads in the complication of daily living, time spent in **praise** and **thanksgiving** will help us overcome our sense of helplessness. It truly is a "sacrifice of **praise** to God" when we are praising with a broken heart or under difficult and challenging circumstances. My strength came in remembering "God inhabits the **praises** of His people and **praise** dispels the enemy." Regardless of the circumstances, we can **praise** the Lord and rejoice in Him.

> God inhabits the **praises** of His people and **praise** dispels the enemy.

Depending on the circumstances we are going through, there are times we might find ourselves **dis**couraged, **dis**appointed, **dis**satisfied, **dis**heartened, or dealing with some other 'dis' that influences us. God wants us to be happy. Offering Him moments of **adoration** provides the opportunity to take our eyes off ourselves and focus completely on Him. "If you have trouble **praising** God with a song in your heart as you serve Him, it may be that your focus is not on God, but on your circumstances."[72] This is the time to rest in His presence. As we **exalt** God, we will be invigorated by His Spirit.

Scripture tells us, *It came even to pass, as the trumpeters and singers were as one, to make one sound to be heard in **praising** and **thanking** the Lord; and when they lifted up their voice with the trumpets, and cymbals, and instruments of music, and **praised** the Lord, saying, "For He is good; for His mercy endureth forever; that then the house was filled with a cloud, even the house of the Lord; so that the priests could not stand to minister by reason of the cloud, for the glory of the Lord had filled the house of God.*[73]

Oh that the glory of the Lord would fill *our* house! From this passage it is clear if we want God's presence to abide in our home, we need to start **praising** and offering our expressions of **gratitude**. If anyone is worthy of **praise** it is our God, our Savior! We need to remember to **praise** God under any and all circumstances. "**Praise** is rooted not in the circumstances of the moment but in the nature and trustworthiness of God."[74] "Our Father can change a seemingly unfortunate situation to a **praiseworthy** situation. There is immeasurable power in **praise**!"[75] Educate yourself to have unlimited confidence in God. Wait patiently.

When I was struggling to understand how to offer **adoration** to our Father, I turned to the Psalms. One of my favorites is Psalm 145. As I reflected on these inspiring passages, words of **adoration** and **praise** surfaced with joy from my heart filled with **gratitude**. It seems incredible God is willing to use us in His service, in spite of our blunders, when the angels could do His bidding in half the time, with much more success. His pardoning grace, His unconditional love, His willingness to risk our rejection and disobedience, His continual generosity, all offer substance for awesome reflection and heartfelt **acclamation**.

After writing the above paragraph I lay down and reflected on the words. I thought, I have a warmth, a thrill, from all this love I feel inside me towards the Trinity. I am sometimes unable to put into words the depth of my devotion, appreciation and awe. All this I feel because God first loved me. These feelings infiltrate my thinking because, even in my deepest heartaches and discouraged confusion, He has been there working on my behalf; arranging things to prepare me for eternity. He always comes through, even after periods of seeming silence. I love each member of the Godhead; the Father, Son and Holy Spirit. Though I have never seen Them, I have felt Them and experienced Them. I express adoration by saying "I love you Lord, because ..." or "God, You are ...."

It's rather like falling in love with a pen pal; a pen pal who somehow keeps up with all your needs and desires and is one step ahead of you offering encouragement, counsel, protection and surprise gifts. You haven't a clue as to what he looks like, but he has won your heart. You know you would be accepted, secure, protected, and loved so it no longer matters what he looks like. You have found a good thing and you're not going to let go of it.

Intimacy develops after we have learned to trust. Through deep, heart-sharing communication we become cherished friends. We recognize each other's value. The more we reflect on their specialness to us, contemplating their specific qualities, the more we desire to be in their company.

That is how it is with God. That's why taking time to **adore** Him and **thank** Him are so important for us. It helps us remember how very blessed we are, and how very trustworthy and capable He is. It helps us be more receptive of His direction and involvement in our lives.

Prayer should begin with **praise. Praise** from a **thankful** heart opens us to God's presence. Christians can grow to the point where they are **thankful** for everything, even the trials and disappointments. If we trust God, there is no reason to remain downcast. He assures us *all things work together for good to them that love God, to them who are called according to His purpose.*[76] It should be enough to provoke our thanks that Jesus called us into existence, loves us, and He had a plan in advance for our salvation and eternal life. Our prayers of **praise** and **thanksgiving** change us from the inside.

At each meal we say our blessing and **thank** God for our food. Are our utterances of **thanksgiving** heartfelt or have they become routine? Paul's letter to the Philippians is an epistle of **thanksgiving**, filled with rejoicing, reminding us to *Rejoice in the Lord always,*[77] giving **thanks** *always for all things to God and the Father in the Name of our Lord Jesus Christ.*[78] The highest form of prayer is that of **adoration** and **thanksgiving**. It is a joyous way of lifting our spirits and declaring our love and loyalty to Him. A **thankful** heart ... **praises!**

May God help us to never speak one word of complaint or go around grumbling, but to instead be refreshed by a heart of **thankfulness** in His presence contemplating our blessings. "Let only **praise** and **gratitude** be the language of our hearts."[79]

Hindrance:

The opposite of **praise**, **adoration**, and **thanksgiving** would be an unthankful and complaining spirit.

Assignment:

Answer the following questions:

How have you shown your lack of appreciation to God?

What have you grumbled or complained about lately?

What is your focus of dissatisfaction?

For the next ten days, in your journal write down ten dif-ferent things each day you are **thankful** for. **Praise** God each day for them. Begin your devotional time **praising** and **adoring** God.

Derry says:
Come on, you can do it. Swallow
your pride. Walk in peace.

TEMPTATION, REPENTANCE, CONFESSION AND RESTITUTION

*Search me, O God, and know my heart: try me, and know
my thoughts: and see if there be any wicked way in me,
and lead me in the way everlasting.*
—Psalm 139:23,24 KJV

I CAN REMEMBER when my son came to me complaining about pain in his thumb. It appeared he had an abscess filled with infection. I suggested it be lanced so it could begin the healing process. He differed in his opinion. Since he was over 18 and responsible for his decisions, he waited. Two days later things looked pretty serious. Fortunately, a doctor from church saw it and insisted my son come to his home so it could be taken care of. It was so bad, our friend had to dig very deep to find the core cause. A large pus pocket was beginning to congeal. How much pain and discomfort my son could have been spared if he had tended to the problem when it first manifested itself.

We sometimes do that same thing with sin. We don't want the discomfort of giving up something that is poisoning our body or mind. We decide not to deal with it. The next thing we know the infectious sin has spread and is causing radiating pain and discomfort to us and those closest to us. We need to visit the Master Physician and let Him perform whatever surgery is needed so the healing process can begin.

The command, *Watch therefore, and pray always, that you may be counted worthy to escape all these things that will come to pass, and to stand before the Son of Man*[80] is also a promise. To watch and pray will be the duty of every Christian until Jesus returns. With total confidence we can feel secure in the truth that God never asks us to do anything He is not willing to help us do. When we call out for strength to resist **temptation** our prayers are immediately answered, but we are expected to remove ourselves from that which causes the **temptation**. "The enemy cannot overcome the humble learner of Christ, the one who walks prayerfully before the Lord ..."[81] It is far easier to resist **temptation** than to live with the consequences.

> ... God never asks us to do anything He is not willing to help us do.

Sometimes we are unaware we are living in sin or have developed sinful habits. To prevent living with this 'blind spot' in our lives, it would be well for us to echo the prayer David prayed in Psalm 139:23 and Psalm 19:12 NASB, *Search me, O God and know my heart: try me, and know my thoughts: and see if there be any wicked way in me, and lead me in the way everlasting. Who can discern his errors? Acquit me of hidden faults.* God's repeated warnings are clear: *If I **regard** iniquity in my heart, the Lord will not hear me.*[82]

This does not mean to say *if* we have sin in our life. We are all sinners and come short of the glory of God. This verse is referring to those cherished sins in our life, those sins we attempt to hide, that we know have a hold on us, but we are not willing to let go of. Sins we hang on to because we enjoy them.

Sometimes we are not as aware as we should be, in relating to other people. About 15 years ago I was personally reminded of this, when a well-meaning lady let me know I

76

was not listening to the wishes of those around me. Her admonition had a transforming effect on me. As I pondered her rebuke, I reflected on other situations where I had heard but not listened. The Lord used that correction to bring to light an incident within my own family.

My son, during his childhood, would always tell me he did not want a birthday party. I felt trapped. I thought, if I don't do anything, he will think I don't love him. If I do something for him, he seemed upset and unappreciative. I was never sure what to do so I decided I would err on the side of generosity. I would make sure there was some kind of celebration planned. With seven sons you have a party with just the family present! If I had really listened, I could have validated my son more effectively. The problem was I hadn't heard his heart.

After further reminiscing, I was convinced I needed to talk to my son and apologize, even though it was many years later and he was no longer living at home. When I called and asked for his forgiveness, he found it difficult to keep his composure. I realized for all these years he had been carrying pain due to my insensitivity. How grateful I am the Lord allowed an uncomfortable situation for me to initiate and affect an area of healing in my relationship with my son. Sometimes we love people the way we want to love them, or in a way that is comfortable for us, instead of the way they need to be loved.

> Sometimes we love people the way we want to love them, or in a way that is comfortable for us, instead of the way they need to be loved.

Recognizing and accepting we aren't perfect, that *we* could indeed be a large part of a problem, can be difficult; but it's the first step. *If we say that we have no sin, we deceive ourselves, and the truth is not in us. If we **confess** our sins, He is faithful and just to forgive us our sins and cleanse us from all unrighteousness.*[83] We all want to have people think we are okay. Far better it is though, to let God reveal those areas in our life where we need to direct a little concentrated effort towards improvement. None of us is perfect. We all have problem areas.

How wonderful it would be if we would support others while they are growing, and not demand from them the perfection we have not yet achieved for ourselves. We should be open to growth in areas that are pointed out to us. This does not mean we should try to please everyone. God does not want us to be people-pleasers. *For do I now persuade men, or God? Or do I seek to please men? For if I still pleased men, I would not be a bondservant of Christ.*[84]

We need to weigh honestly what others bring to our attention, because the problem might not be ours, but theirs.

Unconfessed sin is a barrier between us and God. **Confession** should be specific and heartfelt. "True **confession** is always of a specific character, and acknowledges particular sins. They may be of such a nature as to be brought before God only; they may be wrongs that should be **confessed** to individuals who have suffered injury through them; or they may be of a public character, and should then be publicly **confessed**. But all **confession** should be definite and to the point, acknowledging the very sins of which you are guilty."[85] Recognition of our sin, **repentance**, **confession**, and requesting forgiveness, are sometimes not all that is needed. We can ask God to forgive us, but we must do so with a plan of **restitution** if it is needed. If we have stolen, God requires us to pay back with interest.[86] If we have taken part in character assassination, we must do all we can to undo the wrong committed and attempt to restore the person to right relationship with others. Many prayers remain unanswered because of an unwillingness to bring resolution to past sins that God brings to our mind.

Some sins **confessed** should be only for God's ears. To speak them to anyone else could bring unnecessary and irreconcilable heartache. There is a time to speak and a time to be silent.

While it is important to accept the fact that **confessing** our sins does not necessarily mean there will be no consequences, we are also assured "It is God's glory to encircle sinful, **repentant** human beings in arms of His love, to bind up their wounds, to cleanse them from sin, and to clothe them with the garments of salvation."[87]

Our personal worship time with God should include time in **confession**. It should be a warning to us if we are not in the habit of **repenting** and **confessing** our sins. God wants us to be specific in our requests and in our **confessions**. We should go before the Father and **repent**, asking Him to reveal our blind spots, *for all have sinned and fall short of the glory of God.*[88] "He waits with unwearied love to hear the **confessions** of the wayward to accept their **penitence**."[89]

Behold Christ. Dwell upon His love and mercy. This will fill the soul with abhorrence for all that is sinful and will inspire it with an intense desire for the righteousness of Christ. The more clearly we see the Savior, the more clearly shall we discern our defects of character. **Confess** your sins to Christ and with true contrition of soul, cooperate with Him by putting these sins away. Believe that they are pardoned. The promise is positive, *If we* **confess** *our sins, He is faithful and just to forgive us our sins, and to cleanse us from all unrighteousness.*[90] "Be assured that the word of God will not fail. He who has promised is faithful. It is as much your duty to believe that God will fulfill His word and forgive you as it is to **confess** your sins ..."[91] "To be saved means to be liberated from our sins, freed from our fear of death, and then given the gift of sublime companionship with the Savior."[92]

What if we feel our sins are so terrible that even though we confess them, we wonder whether God has accepted us and if they are really behind us?

Our Savior is so gracious, so aware of how sin affects us and scars our heart, He came up with a plan to remind us that He died so we might have life; that our sins are forgiven.

First, He exemplified the necessity and power of baptism. Baptism symbolizes that we have been buried with Christ and resurrected a new creation. All our sins have been washed away. God's word says in 2 Corinthians 5:17, *Therefore, if anyone is in Christ, he is a new creation; old things have passed away; behold, all things have become new. Now all things are of God, Who has reconciled us to Himself through Jesus Christ ...*

But after that wonderful day of cleansing and new beginnings, we sin again. Then what? Once again we go before the Father and confess our sins with a repentant heart. He knows we will slip or fall short, so He provides us a special service, the Lord's Supper, also called the Communion Service. This is a time of cleansing, a washing away, a time of new beginnings. It is also symbolic of Christ's death and resurrection, which was for the forgiveness of sin.

The preparatory service is self-examination, and any confession, repentance and reconciliation that needs to be tended to. God wants us to have things right between our brethren and us, so He has exemplified the foot-washing service. You can read about this service in John 13 beginning with verse 12.

In 1 Corinthians 11:24-31 He has instructed us to take unleavened bread to symbolize his body broken and sacrifice for us, and wine (pure juice of the vine—grape juice) to symbolize the shedding of His blood. It was His sacrifice and victory over sin that was given for us that we might *live life and live it more abundantly,* looking forward to eternity with Him. Jesus says, *Do this in remembrance of Me.* It is also our reminder of the hope we have to spend eternity with Him.

Remember, 1 John 1:9 says, *If we confess our sins, He is faithful and just to forgive us our sins, and to cleanse us from all unrighteousness.* Why wait? You can have peace of mind and heartfelt joy if you get everything behind you. His sacrifice is enough for the worst possible sin. Do you need to see someone about baptism? Do you need to confess Christ as your Savior? Perhaps you have been baptized; then you can look forward to your next Communion Service to symbolize your heart's desire. You don't have to wait to have everything right with God, though. Moment by moment you can come to Him and be cleansed, asking for His forgiveness. May God bless you as you come before God humbly asking for your "cleansing" or "purification."

For God so loved the world that He gave His only begotten Son, that whoever believes in Him should not perish but have everlasting life.—John 3:16.

Hindrance:

Cherished sin—*If I had cherished iniquity in my heart, the Lord would not have listened.*—Psalm 66:18 ESV

Assignment:

Contemplate the following questions and take whatever action is necessary.

In what areas of my life am I most vulnerable to **temptation**?

Do I have any **unconfessed** sins? What are they?

Do I have any unresolved issues with anyone? With
whom? And What?

Do I need to make **restitution**? If so, what is my plan to
do that?

Have I talked to God, requesting His forgiveness and wisdom to take care of any pending issues?

"What we need is to see clearly how the Father leads His waiting, teachable child to know that his petition is according to His will."
—Andrew Murray,
With Christ in the School of Prayer

PART THREE

"Those who exercise but little faith now, are in the greatest danger of falling under the power of satanic delusions and the decree to compel the conscience. And even if they endure the test they will be plunged into deeper distress and anguish in the time of trouble, because they have never made it a habit to trust in God. The lessons of faith which they have neglected they will be forced to learn under a terrible pressure of discouragement. We should now acquaint ourselves with God by proving His promises."
—Ellen G. White,
The Great Controversy

Derry says:
Play detective and start your
investigation.

Prayer of Faith/
Prayer of Reception

... with Your mouth You have promised and with Your hand
You have fulfilled it ...
　　　　　　　—2 Chronicles 6:15 NIV

WHEN THE PASTOR showed up at my door unexpect-
edly and offered to teach me about the Prayer of
Faith, I was suspicious, but enthusiastic. He was
taking a class called *The Positive Way*, and his assignment
that week was to teach someone else what he had learned
so far. He told me through presenting scripture to God for
His fulfillment, I would soon develop a personal relationship with my Lord. I wanted that. I had never understood
God was really there for me. I somehow thought miracles
were only for missionaries across the sea. I will be forever
grateful to Bob and Elsie Law for this dynamic class of *The
Positive Way* that has changed my life and perspective of
God over 30 years ago. Truly God is a personal God Who
loves you and me. He is anxious to prove Himself to each
of us. Knowing this truth makes all the difference in how
we respond to life.

I soon learned in order to pray the Prayer of **Faith**, or
Prayer of **Reception** as it is also called, I had to become
acquainted with God's word so I could recognize His prom-

ises and commands. I also learned every command is a promise; for God never asks us to do anything He is not willing to help us do. As we study the promises and commands, *we have prayer material,* and we learn what the will of God is. The promises of God provide us subject matter for prayer. Presenting God's pledged word assures us of its fulfillment. Prayer of **Faith** requires just that—**faith,** as well as obedience. "Prayer and **faith** are closely allied, and they need to be studied together. In the Prayer of **Faith**, there is a *divine science;* it is a science that every one who would make his lifework a success must understand."[93] We are to understand "that the gift is in the promise."[94] "Whatever gift He promises, is in the promise itself. The seed is the word of God. As surely as the oak is in the acorn, so surely is the gift of God in His promise. If we receive the promise, we have the gift."[95]

> As we study the promises and commands, *we have prayer material,* and we learn what the will of God is.

> "God stands back of every promise that He has made and the honor of His throne is staked for fulfillment of His Word to us."

"It is part of God's plan to grant us, in answer to the Prayer of **Faith** that which He would not bestow did we not thus ask."[96] "God stands back of every promise that He has made and the honor of His throne is staked for fulfillment of His Word to us."[97]

An effective prayer life is linked to **faith**. Exercising both our **faith** and prayer communication together, bring us into a closer relationship with our Lord. *For by grace are ye saved through **faith**; and that not of yourselves: it is a gift of God.*[98]

James 4:2 tells us *We have not because we ask not.* God does not respond to our prayers if we are unwilling to do our part. God does not encourage us to expect something for nothing. We need to watch and pray; obey and pray, knowing that God will answer our prayers for our best

good ... even if that means withholding for our best interest.

Throughout the *Bible*, God's promises are made under
varying circumstances. His promises provide assistance
and blessings for our life, here and now, as well as for our
eternal future. He wants us to know there is no need so
great or problem so big He cannot provide. God's word
tells us specifically to hold fast to God's promises. Our
most important needs are
not for material things, but
for spiritual guidance and a
Christ-like character.

Our most important needs are
not for material things, but for
spiritual guidance and a Christ-
like character.

*Whereby are given unto us, exceeding great and precious
promises, that by these ye might be partakers of the divine
nature having escaped the corruption of the world ...*[99]
Even though we read "by these promises" and through
these promises, it needs to sink in to the innermost part of
our being that God is anxious for us to learn and incorporate the Prayer of **Faith**. By taking the word of God and
presenting it back to Him, **fulfilling the conditions** and
believing with thanksgiving, He is willing to open the
windows of heaven on our behalf. Understanding them
and applying them is foundational to experiencing God's
intimacy in your life.

The **conditions** will be addressed separately in the following chapters.

Assignment:

This week, pick up another journal to use as your "Prayer Journal."

If you knew you could ask God for anything, what would it be? Search your heart and make a list. Consider more than material things.

Derry asks:
Are you anxious to follow God's
directions or will you ignore them?

OVERVIEW OF CONDITIONS
FOR ANSWERED PRAYER

"It is tragic that Satan is able to keep Christians in such bondage because they have not been taught what really belongs to them as joint heirs with Christ."
—Dr. Hobart Freeman,
Positive Thinking and Confession

THE FOLLOWING COULD BE looked at as a natural progression of spiritual growth. The steps in bold highlight promises in scripture that are also general **conditions** we will be studying in detail in the forthcoming chapters. They should actually become a regular part of our life. They are not difficult. You are probably living most of them out without realizing the importance God places on them, or that He names them as **conditions**. God asks; He enables. The bottom line is "we have not, because we ask not" (or maybe we just don't need it).

God's word is powerful. He wants us to take advantage of His willingness to empower us and bless us. If we do not **feel our need** of God, we obviously won't be spending our time studying scripture to determine His will, or accept His direction, encouragement or correction of our actions contrary to His desires. So before we claim any promise, it makes sense we must **feel our need** of **help from God**.

91

As our heart opens to God, we come **asking**. Asking in the blessed **Name of Jesus** gives our prayers efficacy. It is only by Jesus' name we have access to the Father; not just by His name, but with His heart and spirit. *He who did not spare His own Son, but gave Him up for all of us—how will He not also, along with Him, graciously give us all things?*[100]

Jesus invites us to **ask, believing** we will receive the answer, and to **give thanks** in all things. How do we know if what we are asking for is according to God's will? We study scripture and become acquainted with the promises. This reveals God's heart and what He wants to bestow on us—His children. We can even ask Him what He wants us to pray for.

We become **persevering** and **diligent** in our search for the promises and in our presentation of them to our Father. As we **persevere** we find we must **patiently** wait upon God—**without doubting**. (If we do struggle with doubt or unbelief, there is even a promise in scripture found in Mark 9:24 we can claim for help: *Lord, I believe. Help Thou my unbelief.*) It is as we **seek God** and **His righteousness** we are assured He will provide for all our needs.

The more we seek Him and learn of Him, the more we long to **turn from our evil ways, surrender** our heart to Him and walk in **obedience**. We pray for the **infilling of the Holy Spirit**, Who convicts us and brings us to a point of **repentance**. Now we **confess** before Him, ask for **forgiveness**, making **restitution** as possible. As we **forgive** ourselves and others, we find our heart is more open to **love**. The more we love—God and others—the more we are able to show **mercy, blessing** others and showing **concern** for them. This will promote our **intercession** for them. In our growing **faith**, we **trust, holding fast our confidence** in God with **humility**.

Following this line of instruction, it is just as important we examine scripture where God accentuates specifically; under certain circumstances He will *not* hear us, listen to us or answer our prayers. This is something we don't generally like to look at, but we want to be sure there is nothing between God and us that would prevent Him from communicating with us or answering our prayers. I have included a section on "Hindrances to Answered Prayer" for clarification.

As we study scripture we see God's plan revealed. He wants us to reflect Christ's character—to love with Jesus' love, forgive with Jesus' forgiveness, and become partakers of His divine nature. We need to appropriate these in our life. If we claim God's promises, we **should** see change exhibited in our life. This takes commitment, well worth the time and effort invested. The rewards are now and eternal.

In the chapters following, you will find instructions as to how to apply the promises and **conditions** to your own life. The **conditions** taught are general **conditions; conditions** that would apply, in general, to all promises we want to claim. There are however, additional **conditions** you will find attached to particular promises that must be acknowledged as well.

For example, let's look at the promise in Malachi 3:10. The **condition** for the blessing is that we bring our tithes into the storehouse. God says *if we do*, He will open the windows of heaven and pour out a blessing so big we will not have room enough to receive it. As we read and study the promises, we must study them carefully to see if God has additional expectations we need to comply with.

This method of praying is with your *Bible* open and is not to take the place of heart-sharing communication with God. It is to enhance your prayer experience, insuring a growing love and understanding for God and a desire for Kingdom dwelling. "We should not present our petitions to God to **prove** whether He will fulfill His word, but **because** He will fulfill it; not to prove that He loves us, but because He loves us."[101] God knows the sincerity and desires of

93

the heart, and will answer in His way, in His time. Let us not restrict God's blessings by lack of faith or disobedience.

"Faith that enables us to receive God's gifts is itself a gift, of which some measure is imparted to every human being. It grows as exercised in appropriating the word of God. In order to strengthen faith, we must often bring it in contact with the word."[102]

... follow God's way, and work in conjunction with Him—living your life *Praying in the 'YES' of God.*

For God so loved the world that He gave .... What did He give? God gave what we needed most—our Savior. God longs to give us the desires of our hearts and **will**, if it is not to our detriment. If it is, He will encourage us in our disappointments. There are some prayers we will one day thank God for not answering *our* way. May you become even more victorious and your life more exciting, as you understand and incorporate the **conditions** to answered prayer, follow God's way, and work in conjunction with Him—living your life ***Praying in the 'YES' of God***. May victory be ours through Him!

Assignment:

Answer the following questions:

Was the thought of there being **conditions** a new awareness for you?

Which **conditions** are you already fulfilling in your daily
life?

Which **conditions** need to be incorporated into your life?

"The purpose of prayer is not to convince God to change your circumstances but to prepare you to be involved in God's activity."
—Henry T. Blackaby,
Experiencing God Day by Day

Derry says:
It's as simple as 1, 2, 3.

Prayer of Faith: Verbal Conditions for Answered Prayer

And whatsoever things you ask in prayer, believing, you will receive.
— Matthew 21:22

WE ARE BEGINNING OUR exploration of the **conditions** that need to be fulfilled, in Christ's promised strength, if we are to expect answers to the **Prayer of Faith**. In this chapter we will concentrate on the three *verbal* conditions: **ask**, **believe**, and **thank God that you have received.** Later we will explore other general **conditions** as well as those attached to particular promises.

"For the pardon of sin, for the Holy Spirit, for a Christ-like temper, for wisdom and strength to do His work, for any gift He has promised, we may **ask**: then we are to **believe** that we receive and **return thanks** to God that we have received."[103] When we understand God's promises, and the **conditions** upon which they will be fulfilled, we are seldom disappointed once we apply them. God wants us to work in partnership with Him. That will take commitment and investment: investment of heart, mind and time.

97

The first verbal **condition** is that we **Ask**. *If you abide in Me, and My words abide in you, you will **ask** what you desire, and it shall be done for you.*[104] That seems simple enough. But how many of us don't **ask** because we don't feel like we deserve it or we don't want to bother the Lord. Maybe we are afraid to **ask** because we have been let down and hurt by so many people; that we are afraid if God does not answer, we will have nothing to put our faith in; that possibility is overwhelming to us. It just isn't worth the risk. Oh that Christ Himself, would be our heart desire, rather than anything He could give us or do for us. *Delight yourself also in the Lord; and He shall give you the desires of your heart.*[105] We are invited to **ask**—not *demand.* "He makes it plain that our **asking must be according to God's will**, we must **ask** for the things He has promised, and whatever we receive must be **used in doing His will**. The **conditions** met, the promise is unequivocal."[106]

Does this then mean you can request a second home or some luxurious desire to be fulfilled? I suppose you can, if the primary purpose is for Kingdom glory. Only God would know the intentions of your heart. In general, this is referring to our basic needs, be they physical, material, emotional, or spiritual. (Prayer for healing will be addressed in Part 4, "Commitment.")

God already knows what we have need of and is anxious to open the windows of heaven on our behalf. *Then you shall call and the Lord will answer, you shall cry, and He will say, Here I am.*[107]

Asking God is an expression of trust and of dependence on Him; an admission we cannot manage without Him. How is it we are willing to believe God for our salvation, but have such difficulty trusting Him when it comes to forgiveness issues or providing for our needs? He is able and willing to help us in the least as well as the greatest. "That you feel and know you are a sinner is sufficient ground for asking for His mercy and compassion. The condition upon which you may come to God is not that

you shall be holy, but that you desire Him to cleanse you
from all sin and purify you from all iniquity."[108]

Next, we are admonished to **Believe**. *Jesus said unto him,
If you can* **believe**, *all things are possible to him who* ***believes***.[109] **Believe** God can do through you what you cannot, and He can enable you if you are willing. It is God's
desire that our joy be full. He wants to fill our dreams. In
fact, if we are walking with Him, it is God Who plants the
dream within our heart. The talents He has given us He
desires to incorporate in our daily life that we might experience fullness of joy and be a blessing to those we are
in contact with. "Whenever God reveals something, He expects us to **believe** Him and adjust our lives accordingly."[110]

After we ask, we wait; believing. If we are having difficulty believing, we can say as did the father of the demon-possessed boy in Mark 9:24, *Lord, I* ***believe***. *Help
Thou my* ***unbelief***.

Thirdly, God requests we show our trust and appreciation
by offering a word of **Thanks**. *Giving* ***thanks*** *always for all
things unto God and the Father in the name of the Lord Jesus Christ*.[111] *Pray without ceasing. In everything give*
thanks; *for this is the will of God in Christ Jesus concerning you*.[112]

We can **thank** God in advance because as soon as we ask,
He begins working on the fulfillment of the promise. The
Bible says, *Be careful for nothing, but in everything by
prayer and supplication with* ***thanksgiving***, *let your requests be made known unto God*.[113] (See the chapters on
"Perseverance and Diligence," and "Faith, Obedience and
Patience" regarding delay in answered prayers.)

Answers are sometimes different than what we **request**,
but God will do for us *abundantly more than we* ***ask*** *or
think*.[114] Consider Moses, who **asked** permission to cross

the Jordan. God took Moses directly home to heaven to dwell with Him instead![115] Another good example is King Solomon, when he **asked** for wisdom. God granted him wisdom *and* honor.[116] What a shame we limit God. He may have in mind to give us far more than we **ask**. "God has more prepared for us than we are prepared to **ask**. We need to spend as much time seeking what God wants us to **ask** for as we do **asking**. Then our **asking** will be in keeping with His will."[117]

"You will never set a goal so big or attempt a task so significant that God does not have something far greater that He could do in and through your life."

"You will never set a goal so big or attempt a task so significant that God does not have something far greater that He could do in and through your life ... Until we have heard from God, we cannot even imagine all that our lives could become or all that God could accomplish through us. We need to remind ourselves that the Father sees the 'big picture,' that His power far exceeds our limited imagination."[118] "Follow the Savior's example and let your time alone with God in prayer, set the agenda for your life."[119]

Look for God to answer at a time, and in a way, that we least expect. He is a fun Father Who loves surprises. Let us bring ourselves in accordance with God's will, spend time in our *Bibles*, searching the Word that we may be sure we are following the directions given—for our own sakes, and for our own peace of mind.

Instructions:

How we pray the Prayer of Faith:
- We **Ask**: "For any gift that He has promised we are to **ask**.
- We **Believe**: Then we are to **believe** that we receive, and
- We **Thank**: return **thanks** that we have received."[120]

Here is an example of how to incorporate this prayer:

For the Holy Spirit (promise found in Luke 11:13), we turn to that promise in the *Bible* and we can say,

> Dear Heavenly Father,
>   I **ask** that You give me the Holy Spirit.
>
>   I **believe** You are giving me the Holy Spirit because You have promised in Luke 11:13 that You will.
>
>   I **thank** You that You *have* given me the Holy Spirit.

Assignment:

This week the important focus is to begin to find promises applicable to your needs or the needs of your loved ones and familiarize yourself with the above prayer method.

Begin to list problems and pertinent promise texts on the following page. You may refer to the list of promises at the back of the book in Appendix B, to get you started.

Say the prayer for the Holy Spirit above in your own words, including the three verbal **conditions**, **ask**, **believe** and **thank God you have received**, until it becomes a comfortable part of your prayer time.

Record of Experiences

On the next two pages, the Record of Experiences will help you keep a list of the problems you had, the promises you claim and the date your prayers were answered. It will help to increase your faith in the future when you can look back and see how God so miraculously intervened.

Note: An additional copy of these "Record of Experiences" pages can be found in the back of this book for you to photocopy, and is also available for download on our website at: **FreedomInSurrender.net**

Record of Experiences

This record of experiences will help you keep a list of the problems you had, the promises you claimed and the date your prayers were answered. It will help to increase your faith in the future when you can look back and see how God so miraculously intervened.

Date Asked	Problem	Promise Text	Date Answered	How Answered

"There is a way to ensure that you prosper in
what you do: serve the Lord with all your heart!"
—Henry T Blackaby,
Experiencing God Devotional

Record of Experiences

This record of experiences will help you keep a list of the problems you had, the promises you claimed and the date your prayers were answered. It will help to increase your faith in the future when you can look back and see how God so miraculously intervened.

Date Asked	Problem	Promise Text	Date Answered	How Answered

"Follow the Savior's example, and let your time alone with God, in prayer, set the agenda for your life."
—Henry T Blackaby,
Experiencing God Devotional

Derry says:
You can do it on your own or you
can go into partnership with God.

Prayer of Faith Condition: Feel Our Need

... Jesus said to them, "It is not the healthy who need a doctor, but the sick. I have not come to call the righteous, but sinners."

—Mark 2:17 NIV

AFTER 22 YEARS I couldn't believe I had listened to my husband's confession again, had witnessed his impatience with my inability to accept his secondary lifestyle, and now the silence of the house; silence interrupted by my cries of anguish.

"If ever I **needed** you Lord, it is now," I sobbed. "I **need** Your strength. I **need** Your protection. I **need** Your provision. I **need** to be able to love with Your love and forgive with Your forgiveness. I **need** abundant wisdom, and at this moment more than anything else, I **need** Your comfort, to know You have not abandoned me, too. I cried out with David, *Lord You have promised to perfect what concerns me and not to forsake me.*[121] *My flesh and my heart fail, but God is the strength of my heart and my portion forever.*[122] And I pledged as did Job, *Though You slay me, yet will I serve You.*[123]

107

We **need** to feel our **need** of God. Going through the intense pain and adjustments of being alone was difficult even with God holding me and guiding me. It is difficult for me to imagine the depth of suffering a person would endure going through this on their own.

True to His word, God loved me through. In our opening text Jesus says, *It is not the healthy who need a doctor, but the sick.* Paul reminds us in Romans 3:23, *that all have sinned and come short of the glory of God.* All of us are sinners in **need** of a Savior.

Do you feel the **need** of help from Jesus? I have found I do not want my life to be void of Him. Yes, I **needed** Him when my life fell apart; but I **need** Him every day—during the good times as well as the difficult. *I can do all things through Christ that strengthens me.*[124] That means we trust Him implicitly for all our **needs** because He says He will provide. (Philippians 4:19) "It means we approach crises with the assurance that God will bring good from them."—Romans 8:28[125]

I have just shared with you some very personal and all-encompassing emotional and spiritual **needs**. God has also been there to fill my physical and material **needs** as you will read in following chapters. "The argument that we may plead now and ever is our great **need**, our utterly helpless state, that makes Him and His redeeming power a necessity."[126]

Once we recognize our **need** for Christ, we become more receptive of the idea to spend time communicating with Him. As we open our hearts, sharing becomes easier and we find we are speaking openly to God as to a friend.

Jesus realizes we **need** His help and He is anxious for us to ask so He can step in. Turning to God, in Jesus' name, indicates we recognize our **need**.

I doubt if Jesus cares what the motivating factor is. He just wants us to **need** Him. He is ready to assist us whether it is a life crisis, a **need** for character perfection, or a tangible, momentary **need** we encounter that is in our heart.

Any promise in the *Bible* is indicative of God's heart desire for you; particularly those that deal with character development. He wants to see your character perfected. He is willing to allow you to go through trials, pain, tears, questions and correction to help you come to a positive transition. He will walk through every problem with you. He knows what is on the other side.

Just as those of us who are parents have had to watch our children cry as we exhibit discipline that breaks our heart, we know if we don't administer correction, the end results will not be good. So it is with God. Jesus indicates He will walk with us. He will be so close to us He will taste salt when we cry. He wants us in the Kingdom with Him.

If we relinquish our own desires, make a daily decision to follow God's plan for our life, stop walking the line, and give our all to Jesus, we will discover His all for us. Feeling and knowing our **need** of Jesus is a big first step in understanding the promises are for us and the fulfillment is in Him. God will help it happen. "If your heart is set on pursuing Jesus, you will always find Him."[127]

If your heart is set on pursuing Jesus, you will always find Him.

God would like us to prove for ourselves the reality of His words. His promises will be fulfilled. They have never failed. They never can fail. As we draw near to Jesus we can rejoice in the fullness of His love. When we seek first the Kingdom of God, and **feel** our **need** of Him to control our life, we can be assured that all of our other **needs** will be supplied.[128]

"As you stand in the midst of your confusion with your perspective of life lost, know that I am standing there with you, and I never lose My perspective."—Author unknown.

"There are those who profess to serve God, while they rely upon their own efforts to obey His law, to form a right character, and secure salvation. Their hearts are not moved by any deep sense of the love of Christ, but they seek to perform the duties of the Christian life as that which God requires of them in order to gain heaven. Such religion is worth nothing. When Christ dwells in the heart, the soul will be so filled with His love, with the joy of communion with Him, that it will cleave to Him; and in the contemplation of Him, self will be forgotten. Love to Christ will be the spring of action. Those who feel the constraining love of God, do not ask ... for the lowest standard, but aim at perfect conformity to the will of their Redeemer. With earnest desire they yield all and manifest an interest proportionate to the value of the object which they seek. A profession of Christ without this deep love is mere talk, dry formality, and heavy drudgery."[129]

"All God's biddings are enablings."[130] "Every command is a promise, accepted by the will, received into the soul, it brings with it the life of the Infinite One. It transforms the nature and recreates the soul in the image of God."[131] "In every command or injunction that God gives there is a promise, the most positive, underlying the command."[132]

*Don't worry about anything; instead, pray about everything; tell God your **needs** and don't forget to thank Him for His answers. If you do this you will experience God's peace which is far more wonderful than the human mind can understand. His peace will keep your thoughts and your hearts quiet and at rest as you trust in Christ Jesus.*[133]

Hindrance:

The opposite of "**feeling our need** of Christ" is to "**reject God.**" Read 1 Samuel 8. In verse 18 God says, *you will cry out but the Lord will not answer you.*

Record other key thoughts from this chapter:

Assignment:

Today as you journal, contemplate with God what your **greatest need** is. Find a promise in scripture that applies. List it under 'Promise Text' on the "Record of Experiences" on page 103.

Then, open your *Bible* to that text and incorporate the "**ask**, **believe**, and **thank God that you have received**" principle as you claim the scripture promise for your own.

Claim the promise each day this week.

Share your story. In the space provided below, share your story of how God filled this promise for you and how He filled the condition of **feeling** your **need** of help from Him.

Derry says:
It is only through Jesus that we have access to the Father.

Prayer of Faith Condition: Ask in Jesus' Name

*... Very truly I tell you, My Father will give you whatever you **ask in My name**. Until now you have not **asked** for anything **in My name**. Ask and you will receive, and your joy will be complete.*
—John 16:23-24 NIV

OUR GREAT GOD OF LOVE has stressed the importance of our obedience to conditions He has set forth in regard to prayer and relationship with Him. As we see above, once again the promise is in the condition. Changes of character happen as we fulfill the conditions God has put before us and as we experience His intervention as a result of our specific requests and obedience.

The *Bible* also says *Verily, verily I say unto you, He that believeth on Me, the works that I do shall he do also; and greater works than these shall he do; because I go unto My Father. And whatsoever ye shall **ask in My name**, that will I do, that the Father may be glorified in the Son. If ye shall **ask** any thing **in My name**, I will do it.*—John 14:12-14 KJV. *Jesus said to him, I am the Way, the Truth and the Life. **No one comes to the Father, except through me.**—*John 14:6.

Those are pretty pointed promises, don't you think? Jesus is inviting us to make use of **His name**. That is the condition. So simple. "**Ask in My name**." End your prayers with those words, "*I ask in Jesus' name, Amen.*" I wonder if we realize what it really means to **ask in the name of Jesus**. In my studies, I found when we end our prayers with "*in Jesus' name*" we are acknowledging our acceptance to receive and manifest His character and to work with His given empowerments.

"When with earnestness and intensity we breathe a prayer in the **name** of **Christ**, there is in that very intensity a pledge from God He is about to answer our prayer "exceeding abundantly above all that we ask or think."[134] His name implies love. When we close our prayers acknowledging Him as our only entrance before the Father, we are also praying for the accomplishment of His will on behalf of our request.

> There is no other entrance to heaven except by the name of Jesus.

"Holy and reverend is **His name**," (Psalm 111:9 KJV) the psalmist declares. Angels when they speak that **name**, veil their faces. With what reverence then, should we, who are fallen and sinful, take it upon our lips!"[135] **There is no other entrance to heaven except by the name of Jesus.** It is only because of Jesus sacrificing His life on the cross, and by His atoning blood for sinners like us, that we have access to the Father. "**In the name of Jesus** we may come into God's presence with the confidence of a child. No man is needed to act as a mediator. Through Jesus we may open our hearts to God as to One who knows and loves us." [136]

*You did not choose Me, but I chose you, and appointed you, that you should go and bear fruit, and that your fruit should remain: that whatever you **ask** the Father, in **My name**, He may give you.*[137] *In that day you will **ask in My name**, and I do not say to you that I will ask the Father on your behalf; for the Father Himself loves you, because you have loved Me and have believed that I came from God.*[138]

How awesome! Six times our Savior invites us to pray *in His name* and ask anything we want according to His will. Six times! The wonder of this promise is unimaginable. The Savior gave His life on our behalf; that was the greatest gift. Then He put a bow around that gift by offering us "anything" according to His will. What other gifts could possibly equal these? Does it not make us wonder why we are so little in prayer? Why do we not believe the Savior's words? Why is it so hard for us to depend wholly upon the merits, the invitation, the availability of such a great Father who is willing to open the windows of heaven and pour out the blessings He desires to grant us "according to the riches of His glory," that we may "be strengthened with power through His 'Spirit in the inner man.'" He tells us our strength, our effectiveness, our joy depends upon our prayers—upon our relationship with Him. We are to ask in **Christ's name** *that the Father may be glorified in the Son.*[139]

We are only admonished to conform to God's will, and then we can expect an answer. This is so limitless. Oh, why don't we pray more? Why is it so hard to take God at His word?

We are to ask not for our own glory, but to glorify God. We cannot pray in the **name** of **Jesus** if we are not willing to abide in Him—accepting and desiring to exemplify Christ's character. This changes **"in His name"** from a condition alone, to a way of life. "It is only when whatsoever we do is done **in His name**, that He will do whatsoever we ask, **in His name**."[140] Jesus promises, *I am the Way, the Truth and the Life: no man cometh unto the Father, but by me.*[141]

With a text as direct and specific as the one you just read, how can it be that any pastor or spiritual leader can think to bow before God in front of their congregation and not close their prayer by *asking in Jesus' name*? If we can come to the Father only by and through Jesus, how can we think our prayers will be heard or answered any other way? They will certainly not be if we are coming of ourselves alone. How very important this example is to others.

"As Christ's intercessions in our behalf were heard, the evidence was given to man that God will accept our prayers in our own behalf through the **name of Jesus**."[142]

Assignment:

During this week, pay attention to how God will reveal ways you can more effectively reflect Christ's character. Record these revelations of growth areas as "needs" on the "Record of Experiences" on page 103 and find an appropriate promise to claim to help you make necessary changes. A list of Bible Promises is located in Appendix B.

Continue to claim these promises following the procedure you have been taught with your *Bible* open, but now you will end your prayers "*in Jesus' name*."

Share your story.

My experience: In what ways did God reveal how I can more effectively reflect Christ's character? Record them in the space below.

"If God has not responded to what you are
praying, you may need to adjust your praying
to align with God's agenda."
—Henry T Blackaby,
Experiencing God Day by Day

Derry says:
Hang in there. You're off to a good
start. Don't quit on God.

PRAYER OF FAITH CONDITIONS:
PERSEVERANCE AND DILIGENCE

Praying always with all prayer and supplication in the
Spirit, and watching thereunto with all **perseverance** *and*
supplication for all saints;
                    —Ephesians 6:18 KJV

Looking **diligently** *lest any man fail of the grace of God; ...*
                    —Hebrews 12:15 KJV

THERE ARE ACTUALLY several **conditions** to the above
text, Ephesians 6:18:

- To pray always with all prayer and supplication (pray continually)
- **In the Spirit** (Holy Spirit prompting and intercessions)
- Watching with all **perseverance** and supplication
- **For all saints** (intercession, not just praying for ourselves).

In this chapter we will be addressing **perseverance** and
diligence together to simplify the understanding and interpretation of these two words that are so closely allied.

119

Several years ago my son came into camp concerned. We were at a family Bible camp meeting and not very many young people were showing up for the early-morning worship time. He and a friend of his decided they had to do something to get the kids out for morning worship. Making it a continual matter of prayer, my son began by making an announcement at the evening meeting. He said, "anybody that wants to come for worship, we will go around and wake you up in the morning. Just sign the sheet and list your camp number." The first morning there were only five in the group. The second morning after he made another appeal, there were twelve in the group. My son **persevered**.

He made an announcement the next day. "You know, not very many of you raised your hands or signed up for us to wake you up so you could be at morning worship. Tonight we are looking forward to more of you signing up. We will go around and make sure you are up so you can be there in time. We have girls to wake up the girls and guys to wake up the guys."

With God's blessings, his **diligence** and **perseverance**, in prayer and action, brought 70 young people to early morning worships. So much interest grew, they even added an extra meeting. **Persevering** prayers bring people to Jesus and open them to life-changing possibilities. "Heavenly angels will respond to their self-sacrificing efforts ..."[143]

When we know we are doing God's will and obstacles come up, we can **persevere**. If we move ahead unsure of God's will, we are more tempted to give up. The time to stop **persevering** in prayer is when God says "no" as He did with Paul in 2 Corinthians 12:8-9.

"**Perseverance** and **diligence** may appear to mean the same thing. Word experts, however, indicate there is a distinct difference. **Perseverance** indicates nothing about the quality or quantity of the work accomplished, only the unflagging nature of the effort. **Diligence** suggests the performing of work that is well done and that demands the worker's alertness and dedication to the task."[144] We are counseled that **perseverance** is a condition to receiving. **Perseverance** means to continue resolutely, to be persistent. The *Bible* says, *Pray without ceasing.*[145] "We must pray always if we would grow in faith and experience. We are to be *'instant in prayer'* to *'continue in prayer and watch in the same with thanksgiving.'*—Romans 12:12; Colosians 4:2."[146]

"Hold fast to your Savior as did Jacob, until God shall not only reveal to you yourself but shall reveal to you Himself and you shall see in Jesus a strength and support ... you have never sensed and realized ... If your faith **perseveringly** grasps the promises, you will prevail."[147]

This reminds me of the acronym **PUSH. P**ray **U**ntil **S**omething **H**appens!

God wants us to keep on praying even when we don't see an immediate answer ...

God wants us to keep on praying even when we don't see an immediate answer, resting in the assurance He is working on the answer and we can trust in His timing. We may never know the reason for His delay; but as we wait upon God in trust, our dependence and assurance has opportunity to grow. Only praying people develop faith. God has invited us to ask; ask—not demand, not coax, not bargain. We might even have to agonize until we see lives or circumstances changed or hear God's answer.

Sometimes God seems slow in answering our prayers. Why the delay? It will be for our best good, whether we ever find out why or not. God already knows what our desires and needs are. He has our best interest at heart. Prayer changes us. It changes our attitude, our character and our perspective. It punctuates our inabilities and our total dependence on God. It puts us in a position of deep appreciation when we do receive.

When there are delays our faith might struggle for survival. In the last moments of earth's history we will have to have a faith that endures trials, hardships, hunger, disappointment, discouragement and pain. If we hold fast with the hand of faith when our prayers are not immediately answered, we will learn to hang on in difficult situations where there is no seeming way out lest it come from God. "God is too wise to err, and too good to withhold any good thing from them that walk uprightly."[148]

I have heard people say, "My prayers are never answered." What does that say to us? Well, scripture says, *God is not a man that He should lie*[149] so this can't be about God, or about His word. It would cause me to believe this person needs to learn something about praying. We can all be living a life of continual answers to prayer.

We should never give up too soon. God is a God of love who has our ultimate happiness in mind. He wants us to be prepared for difficult days ahead. We must prove His promises by **diligent**, **persevering** faith and prayers that faint not, doing our part to bring about the fulfillment of our petitions.

Christ is looking for tenacity in our faith that will prevail in spite of delays and setbacks. *Until the time that His word came to pass, the word of the Lord tested him.*[150] The word tests all God's servants before it is fulfilled. In Bible stories we read that for those who kept faith in God during the tests, everything the Lord promised came to pass.

With God all things are possible. It is never a matter of <u>if</u> the word will be fulfilled; but *when*, for the promises in scripture stand. It has been written and it cannot be broken. If God said it, He will do it. If He spoke it, He will make it good.

"Unceasing prayer is the unbroken union of the soul with God, so that life from God flows into our life; and from our life, purity and holiness flow back to God."[151] **Perseverance** and **diligence** in prayer have been made conditions for receiving. "... let nothing hinder you. Make every effort to keep open the communion between Jesus and your own soul."[152] Seek every opportunity to attend and participate where others are gathering to pray. Being together in agreement is empowering and scriptural. *Again I say unto you, That if two of you shall agree on earth as touching any thing that they shall ask, it shall be done for them of my Father which is in heaven. For where two or three are gathered together in My name, there am I in the midst of them.*[153]

The thought of prayer as communion puts it in the light of a habitual attitude and not simply an occasional act. Christ exercised **diligence** in that He would let nothing hinder Him from His time with His Father God, sometimes praying all night. Jesus prayed in public, in His 'family circle,' alone in the mountains, and as He ministered to those around Him So we should join in prayer in the prayer meetings, the family circle, in secret, and as we go about our daily labor. "There is no time or place in which it is inappropriate to offer up a petition to God."[154]

The people who develop this kind of prayer life will have a message to give and a faith to share. It was by earnest, **persevering** prayer that the Holy Spirit was poured out in such abundance on the Day of Pentecost and it is by **diligent** and **persevering** prayer that we will witness miracles in our day. Jesus is coming soon. We must be found active—not sitting and waiting. Even the patient in the sickbed can be actively involved in Jesus' work by interceding for others until their last breath.

Perseverance and **diligence** will always pay off in the end when our efforts are committed to God. Pray and don't faint. God is for us.

Hindrance:

The opposite of "**Perseverance** and **Diligence**" is "**instability**." Read James 1:6-8. Record the message of these texts below.

Assignment:

Continue to find promises in scripture that apply to your own situation, recording them on the "Record of Experiences" on page 103.

Continue to claim these promises following the recommended procedure with your *Bible* open, always ending your prayer "*in Jesus' name*."

Ask God how you can be more **diligent** and **persevering** in your prayer life. What suggestions were revealed?

Find appropriate scripture promises you can claim to activate this change in your life. Record these promises on the "Record of Experiences" on page 103 and claim these promises each day this week.

Share your story: In the space below, record your experience of how God filled this promise for you and is helping you be more **persevering** and **diligent** in prayer.

"Rather than focusing on what you would like to see
happen, realize that God may be more concerned
with what He wants to see happen in you."
—Henry T Blackaby,
Experiencing God Day by Day

PRAYER OF FAITH CONDITION:
SEEK FIRST THE KINGDOM OF GOD

*So do not worry, saying, "What shall we eat?" or "What shall we drink?" or "What shall we wear?" For ... your Heavenly Father knows that you need them. But **seek first His Kingdom** and **His righteousness**, and all these things will be given you as well.*
        —Matthew 6:31-33 NIV

IN THE CHAPTER "Feel Our Need" I shared some personal struggles I had to work through when I faced major crises in my life. During that time God rescued me and responded to my deep emotional pain and spiritual anxieties. In this chapter I share stories that will also affirm for you God's willingness to care for our physical and material needs. The stories following are the direct result of claiming the above promise, to **seek first the Kingdom of God**, and fulfilling the **condition** attached to it.

The evening Pastor Flynn first came to teach me how to personalize scripture and claim God's promises, he had no idea of our financial plight, lack of food, or the urgency of our needs. His visit and this lesson were *very* timely. After his instruction, with the *Bible* open to Matthew 6:33, we claimed this promise and had prayer together.

The next morning I went downstairs to prepare breakfast. Passing the dining room table, I noticed my *Bible* still open to the text we had claimed. In the quietness of the moment I reread Matthew 6:33, *But **seek ye first the Kingdom of God**, and **His righteousness**; and all these things shall be added unto you.* I knelt down, and presented this promise to God. I said, "Lord, I have food for one more meal. If you really care about me and my little boys, I need something to feed them by lunchtime. If You **are** there and if You really hear me, please bring us food. I am fulfilling the condition of this promise and **seeking first Your Kingdom** and **Your righteousness**. You have promised if I do, You will provide for my needs. I believe Your word. I need food for my children by lunchtime. Thank You for sending it."

I got up from my knees wondering what the day would hold. I made breakfast and went about my morning duties, mindful of the clock, and full of anticipation.

Life was difficult. The challenges were overwhelming. Medical problems threatened us financially. We were several months behind in our house payments and facing foreclosure. There was literally one meal left in the cupboard—hot cereal. Would God answer my prayer?

A few minutes before noon, there was a knock at my door. Running to the door with great expectation, I was surprised to see a little grandma whom I had met only once.

Wringing her hands, she said, "I know this might sound a bit strange, but I was at the market this morning and I thought I heard the Lord say, 'Derry needs this and Derry needs that.' Derry, do you need anything?"

"Oh yes. I'm sure that whatever you have, I need."

We unloaded three bags of groceries from her car—enough food for a week. On the top of one bag was even toilet paper and toothpaste. I hadn't thought of that. But God did!!! We were almost out!

God had provided food for us when our cupboards were bare and proved to me we mattered to Him. Now, convinced He was a personal God of love, I decided I needed to be back in church. My second experience with this promise occurred a week later. Claiming again the promise in Matthew 6:33, that if I put Him first, He will provide for my needs—I reminded Him my wardrobe did not have attire suitable for a Christian woman, or for church. Neither did my children. I said, "If we're going to attend church, we need some clothes." I felt a prompting to clean out my closet and trust. So I did.

The next day I received a call from an acquaintance. She said, "Derry, I was just given a pile of clothes and I can't think of anyone I know this size except you. Would you like them?" Would I like them?! I knew they had been sent by God and I couldn't wait to see what He had picked out.

The clothes God sent were nicer than any I had given away. Dresses, skirts, blouses, pant suits, play clothes, nighties, jackets, coats—everything I needed and more. That took care of me, but what about my boys, I wondered. They, too, needed clothes for church.

Two days later I received a phone call from a neighbor a block away. I had not seen her for two years. "I'm desperate," she said. "I have no one to watch my boys for the next few days. Would you be willing?" "I'm happy to help you," I responded.

To my surprise, when she brought her two boys, both a couple of years older than mine, she brought with her a huge plastic garbage bag full of clothes they had outgrown. Three laundry loads full. God supplied both my sons with play clothes, casual clothes, church clothes, jackets and pajamas.

What do you think? Was this just coincidental or did God really hear my petition? I have no doubt! These answers to prayer were the beginning of a new way of life. I now live a life of prayer, adventure and expectation. I have met and know our personal God of love and compassion. When we take one step towards the Savior, He runs all the way to meet us. Daily I feast on God's word claiming His promises. He is a covenant-keeping God. God is anxious for you to know Him and to prove to you He hears and answers your prayers as well.

I like to take the lessons I learn and reflect on Christ. I ask myself that well-known question, "What would Jesus do?" It doesn't take much looking in the gospels to realize Jesus practiced what He preached. From the time He was a child, He was **seeking** Kingdom knowledge. The *Bible* tells us He was so preoccupied in the temple at Jerusalem, sitting among the teachers listening and asking questions, He didn't show up for the journey home. His parents missed Him and had to go looking for Him.

We read that as an adult He got up early in the morning and stayed out late at night to spend time alone with His Father. The time He spent with His Father prepared Him for the demands of each day. God provided for Jesus' needs. He will provide for ours if we also put Him first.

Hindrance:

The opposite of "**Seeking** God" is "**Seeking** other gods."
Read Jeremiah 11:13-14. What does God say He will do?

Assignment:

Continue to find promises in scripture that apply to your
own situation, recording them on the "Record of Experiences" on page 103.

Continue to claim these promises following the recommended procedure with your *Bible* open, always ending
your prayer "*in Jesus' name.*"

Record and claim this week's condition/promise, and expect some excitement. How did God fulfill the promise of
Matthew 6:31-33 in your life this week? Record your story:

"Often we make serious mistakes and then expect God to compensate for our negligence or indifference. Certainly God "knoweth our frame" and "remembereth that we are dust," and He repeatedly comes to our aid in the difficulties that we bring upon ourselves. But we must take care not to try to involve God in endorsing carelessness or disobedience. Often the best thing God can do for us is to let us learn through suffering."
—Edwin R. Thiele,
Knowing God

Prayer of Faith Conditions: Responsive Heart, Humility, Repentance

*Because your heart was **responsive** and you **humbled** yourself before the Lord when you heard what I have spoken against this place and its people, that they would become accursed and laid waste, and because you **tore your robes** and wept in my presence, I have heard you, declares the Lord.*

—2 Kings 22:19 NIV

No TWO DAYS ARE ALIKE ministering as a hospital chaplain. Before I go on duty, I pray God will help me make a difference for His Kingdom's glory. During my devotional time I ask God to help me with a time of heart searching, confession, **repentance** and cleansing from all unrighteousness. Then I ask that He would help me have a sweet and **humble** spirit that **responds** to His voice and **responds** to the needs around me. That He will guide me to those who have a **responsive heart** and give me the words to speak to them.

This particular day I was scheduled to work in the Emergency Room of a large metropolitan hospital. I had been working several hours. The Emergency Room was full.

As I stepped into a patient's room to make a report to the nurse, a cheery voice from the bed greeted me. "Hi." I turned to find a man in his 40s smiling at me.

"What are you doing here," I asked.

"Alcohol" he responded.

"Why?" I questioned.

"I don't know. I love God. I have a wonderful Christian wife and two great children. I don't know. I just can't break the habit."

I sat down next to his bed and asked, "Do you want to break the habit?"

"Oh yes, but I just can't."

We prayed. Then I took out a piece of paper and drew a cross. Just as Pastor Paul Coneff had taught me I began going through the story of Christ from Gethsemane to the crucifixion. I asked the patient to explain in contemporary terminology how he thought Jesus felt and what kind of abuse He had suffered. As we progressed with the story he identified verbal, physical, sexual, emotional, religious, psychological, and satanic abuse.

We came to the part of the story where Jesus said, "I thirst." "Do you remember what they offered Him?" I asked.

"I think it was wine and gall," he said.

"Right! Scripture says in Matthew 27:34 NIV they offered Jesus wine to drink, mixed with gall; but after tasting it, He refused to drink it." Gall refers to bitter herbs, also re-corded as myrrh or wormwood, both pain reducers. Do you know why they offered it to Him?"

"No."

"It was a numbing agent. They offered it to Him to numb the pain. Tradition teaches the women of Jerusalem customarily furnished this pain-killing narcotic to prisoners who were crucified.

"Did Jesus drink it?" I asked him.

"I don't think so. No."

"That's right! Some versions actually say He tasted it but He didn't drink it. When He refused it, it was at that very moment Jesus conquered addictions for all people. Any addiction is about numbing pain and Jesus refused to have His body and mind numbed from pain." The patient began to weep. He said, "I never believed Jesus really understood. Now I know He does."

> I never believed Jesus really understood. Now I know He does.

We talked a while longer and then had prayer. I was about to leave when a young voice on the other side of the curtain called to me. He had overheard my conversation. This 15-year-old boy had been transported by ambulance from his high school because he also suffered from alcohol abuse and had been heavily intoxicated.

This young man had heard me share about the suffering of our Lord. "I want Jesus to help me, too. I want to pray, too. I don't want to live this way any more. I repent before the Lord."

He had never been to church and he didn't know anything about Jesus until now. But with all his heart he embraced the message he had just heard. After praying and sharing, he took off his bandana, the symbol of his gang, and threw it in the trash.

Together we discussed how he would explain to his very angry parents the transformation that had happened during this hospital visit. Before I left, I assured him, "God's power will be imparted as you depend on Him."

135

Before my eyes I experienced a young man **respond**, **repent**, and **humble** himself before the Lord. God in exchange gave him peace of mind and a changed countenance. I'm convinced there is more to the story I will find out someday in heaven.

"When you receive the words of Christ as if they were addressed to you personally, when each applies the truth to himself as if he were the only sinner on the face of the earth for whom Christ died, you will learn to claim by faith the merits of the blood of a crucified and risen Savior.

"Many feel that their faults of character make it impossible for them to meet Christ's standard ... but all that such ones have to do is to **humble** themselves ... under the mighty hand of God."[155] Christ's estimate of us comes from the spirit and intentions of our heart. "When He sees men ... with distrust of self and with reliance upon Him, He adds to their work His perfection and sufficiency, and it is accepted of the Father ... The sinners' defects are covered by the perfection and fullness of the Lord our Righteousness. Those who with sincere will, with **contrite heart**, are putting forth **humble** efforts to live up to the requirements of God, are looked upon by the Father with pitying, tender love; He regards such as obedient children, and the righteousness of Christ is imputed unto them."[156]

Jesus says, *Behold, I stand at the door, and knock: if any man hear My voice, and open the door, I will come in to him, and will sup with him, and he with Me.*[157] He stands at the door and knocks. We have to let Him in. He instructs; we must obey. He says, *Today if you hear His voice, do not harden your hearts.*[158] *Come to Me, all you who are weary and burdened and I will give you rest.*[159] When we **respond**, we are revitalized. Come and rest, *taste and see that the Lord is good.*[160]

How can it be even in America there are so many who have not yet heard about the love of our Savior and the power of the cross? Jesus provides opportunities for those who are willing to share His story. For those who will **humble** themselves and respond with a **true heart** of **repentance**; for those who will listen, Jesus provides answers. *If My people, which are called by My Name, shall* **humble** *themselves, and pray, and seek My face, and* **turn from** *their* **wicked ways***; then will I hear from heaven, and will forgive their sins, and will heal their land.*"[161] "If he seeks the Lord with **humility** and trust, every trial will work for his good."[162]

Hindrance:

The opposite of "**Responsive**" is "**Rebellious**" and the opposite of "**Humility**" is "**Arrogance**." Read Deuteronomy 1:43-45 and Job 35:12-13. Record what God says.

Assignment:

Continue to find promises in scripture that apply to your needs or the concerns of your family and friends, recording them on the "Record of Experiences" on page 103.

Continue to claim these promises following the recommended procedure with your *Bible* open, ending your prayer "*in Jesus' name*."

Record and claim this week's conditions as a promise praying you will be **responsive**, **humble**, and **repentant**.

Are you harboring any anger towards God you need to **repent** of and release?

In what ways has God helped you be **humble**, **responsive** and **repentant** this week? Share your story:

Derry asks:
Will you put aside your will
for His?

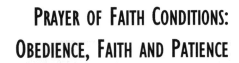

PRAYER OF FAITH CONDITIONS: OBEDIENCE, FAITH AND PATIENCE

Obedience: *Dear friends, if our hearts do not condemn us, we have confidence before God and receive from Him anything we ask, because we **obey** His commands and do what pleases Him.*
—1 John 3:21-22 NIV

Faith: *Without **faith** it is impossible to please God, because anyone who comes to Him must believe that He exists and that He rewards those who earnestly seek Him.*
—Hebrews 11:6 NIV

Patience: *That ye be not slothful, but followers of them who through **faith** and **patience** inherit the promises.*
—Hebrews 6:12 KJV

IT TAKES A LOT OF **FAITH** to rearrange our life and venture forward into previously unexplored vistas. When God first made it clear I was supposed to go back to school and prepare for a degree, I admit I started out less than anxious to obey. I said, "God, I'm almost 50. Are you sure you dialed the right number? Why would You want me to go back to school now?" Providentially, each obstacle was dispelled and the direction defined, except for what degree I was to pursue. That was unclear. To wait **patiently** for clarification was difficult. It was a major step of **faith** to move forward with plans, facing the unknown. I packed my bags, boarded the plane in Sacramento, California, heading for Boston, Massachusetts—the opposite coast—and stepped out in complete **obedience**, that yet lacked understanding. How thankful I was in my daily 'promise-claiming' time I had been praying for stronger **faith**, that I would learn to be 'quick to **obey**' and wait **patiently** for God's timing. God had more in store than I ever could have guessed!

When three days into the program God revealed I was to pursue Chaplaincy, my joy was beyond measure. As a young woman in my twenties, I had worked as a secretary for three chaplains in Los Angeles at White Memorial Hospital. Other than being a wife and mother, it was the joy of my life. I would never have guessed that was what the Lord was calling me into. Unbeknownst to me, God was answering the prayers of my praying community. For four years a group of believers representing about fourteen different denominations had come together and were praying for God to send a chaplain to our community hospital. God was answering their prayers and He was also caring for me. Little did I know, in a very short time I would be facing one of the most difficult heartbreaks and challenges of my life. God was putting me in a position to be able to take care of myself.

God can and will give us the **faith** we need. We are to "lay hold" of the power of Christ. *Have **faith** in God, for verily I say unto you, if ye have **faith** as a grain of mustard seed ye shall say unto this mountain, remove hence to yonder place, and it shall remove, and nothing shall be impossible unto you.*[163] Each of us has been given a *measure of **faith***.[164] The more we exercise it, the stronger it will become.

Many years ago, I had only been exercising the gift of claiming Bible promises for a relatively short time when I was asked to teach what I had learned to a youth group. My **faith** was still a little shaky when I invited this class to come over for dinner after church to share their answered prayers. I'm sorry to have to admit my lack of **faith**. I really didn't expect many to show up. I didn't think the kids were putting into practice what I had been teaching them.

With that attitude, you can imagine my surprise when I saw cars filling my driveway and lining the street half a block away. I panicked! I didn't have enough food for this group. Isn't that awful! Here I was—no food and all these kids!

"We are to seek for that **faith** which works by love and purifies the soul,"[165] sooo, I went to my room and prayed, "Father, I'm sorry for my lack of **faith**. Please forgive me. I'm in big trouble and I need help. You fed the 5000, and I know You can feed these young people, so I'll make You a deal. I'll just send them through the line and I promise I won't look in my crockpot. Would You just keep it full until they're finished?"

I claimed the promise in Matthew 6:26, *Look at the birds of the air: for they neither sow nor reap nor gather into barns; yet your Heavenly Father feeds them. Are you not of more value than they?*

The young people came in. The first few through the line *piled* their plates. I'm sure they thought I had more food than what they saw in that small crockpot. I couldn't believe my eyes. I said, "Okay Lord. I'm not only going to ignore the pot, I'm not even going to look at their plates." So I didn't. I went to the kitchen and waited.

Finally somebody said to me, "Derry, aren't you going to join us?" So I went to the table to fill my plate and looked in the pot. It was half full! Do you understand what I mean? The pot was not half empty, but half full! **Faith** grows—is strengthened, by exercise. God is able to do abundantly, without measure, even today. Jesus loves a party—especially when He is the discussed and praised guest of honor.

Sometimes when I speak at seminars I have been criticized for telling unbelievable stories. That's okay with me. The stories *are* true. As long as God keeps answering prayer I will share my stories about an extraordinary God Who does unbelievable things for us today. Not just in the mission field. Not just years ago—but today, because that's the kind of God He is.

"God's **faithfulness** to His promises should elicit in man **faithfulness** to God and serve as a potent deterrent to a life of sin."[166] Do we take God at His word and accept what He says just as we would do with our other friends? *Whatsoever we ask we receive of Him, because we keep His commandments and do the things that are pleasing to His sight.*[167] God put before Moses and the Israelites the promise of land. But it was **conditional**. **Obedience** brings blessings. Disobedience would bring the loss of the land they had been promised. God warned them, *If in spite of this you do not obey me ... I will make the land desolate ... you I will scatter among the nations.*[168]

"God's timing is perfect! When He speaks, the time to respond in **obedience** is now. We often act as if we have all the time in the world to **obey** Him, but history doesn't wait on our commitments. There is no such thing as postponing a decision with God. Either we **obey**, or we disobey. It is **faith** or unbelief, **obedience** or disobedience.

"When God announces that *now* is the acceptable time, what you do next is critical ... He knows you, and He is fully aware of your circumstances. He knows all that He has built into your life until now, and He extends His invitation knowing that His resources are more than adequate for any assignment He gives you."[169]

Our prayers can never take the place of **obedience** to God. "Those who bring their petitions to God, claiming His promise while they do not comply with the **conditions**, insult Jehovah. They bring the Name of Christ as their authority for the fulfillment of the promise, but they do not those things that would show **faith** in Christ and love for Him."[170]

> Those who bring their petitions to God, claiming His promise while they do not comply with the **conditions**, insult Jehovah.

"That is why Scripture tells us God is concerned with our heart. If we do not keep our heart in love with Jesus, our disobedience when God speaks could affect the lives of others. When God speaks it is always out of the context of eternity. We don't have to know all the implications of what He is asking. We just have to know that it is a word from Almighty God. 'Now' is always the acceptable time to respond to the Lord!"[171]

> When God speaks it is always out of the context of eternity.

We cannot give God half-hearted **obedience**. Our Father wants total heart **obedience**. Jesus, "as the Son of man, gave us an example of **obedience**; as the Son of God He gives us power to **obey**. His life testifies that it is possible for us also to **obey** the law of God."[172] One sign of our being God's friends will be evidenced in our **obedience** to all His commands; not just those that are convenient or tie in with our own thoughts and comfort.

"When our purpose is to know Him, then we no longer *have* to do the "required" thing, but instead we *want* to do the very things which righteousness motivates. Now the disciplines of discipleship become a delight instead of a duty. We desire to do what for most people is a duty. The pressure is off, and the motivation of love is on."[173]

*By **faith** Abraham, when he was called to go out into a place which he should after receive for an inheritance, **obeyed**; and he went out, not knowing whither he went.*[174]

Abraham's **obedience** was a response of **faith**. Abraham's unquestioning **obedience** and trust in God stands as an encouragement and an inspiration. Can you imagine being asked to leave your home and family and go to who knows where? The temptation would be to answer, "You've got to be kidding!"

"If a man stands in a relationship of **faith**, trust, and confidence in God, with its resulting **obedience** to his God, then he is called "righteous.""[175] The *Bible* says, *Understand, then, that those who have faith are children of Abraham ... so those who rely on faith are blessed along with Abraham, the man of faith.*[176] What an example Abraham was. What **patience** he exhibited throughout life waiting for God to make good His promises. When we become discouraged as we wait for God to answer the promises we have claimed, we need to remember **patience** is another **condition** to receiving answers to our prayers.

"Noah responded in **faith, obedience**, and **patience**. His family demonstrated the kind of **obedience**, not whereby man merits anything in the sight of God, but whereby **obedience** issues out of total and complete trust in God."[177] "A stable person established in the gospel can be distinguished by **patience**. He or she knows that God is in charge and is working out His purposes."[178] Noah certainly had to wait **patiently** for the sound of raindrops, didn't he?

> When there are delays our faith sometimes struggles for survival.

One of the sorest trials of our **faith** is petition seemingly unanswered. "When our prayers seem not to be answered, we are to cling to the promise, for the time of answering will surely come, and we shall receive the blessing when we need it most."[179] When there are delays our faith sometimes struggles for survival. It is because sometimes we ask for things that would not be in our best interest. Because God loves us, He gives us not what we are requesting but what is for our best good, and also what we would ask for if we could see with heavenly vision.

144

Faith begins in our moments of secret prayer, in our heart-sharing with Jesus. It is as we come with hearts surrendered to His will, and lay all our petitions at His feet, that our **faith** will have an opportunity to grow and will be rewarded. By **faith** we can claim every promise God has made, knowing Jesus is true to His word.

Just as the Israelites were a chosen, covenant people, so Christians are also covenant people. The New Covenant, however comes to us with far greater promises and unlimited spiritual potential. It was not made directly with us. It was made between the Father and the Son *for us*—two Partners who abide in perfect fulfillment of covenant **conditions**.

The **conditions** for us in the New Covenant are

> This is the glorious wonder of our **faith**: God covenanted with God on our behalf!

markedly different. We access the benefits of the New Covenant through **faith** in God's redemptive work. Our trust is in His works—not ours. This is the glorious wonder of our **faith**: God covenanted with God on our behalf!

"... Our eternal status will be determined on the basis of our **faith** in Christ, His death for our sins and complete trust in His lordship in our lives."[180] We can obtain a **faith** that endures the same way our Savior did; by spending time with the Father, persevering in prayer, trusting, submitting, surrendering to His will, **obeying**, fasting and waiting. Only praying people develop **faith**. "Educate yourself to have unlimited confidence in God. Wait **patiently** and He will bring it to pass. We must keep the heart open if we would receive the grace of God."[181] **Faith**, **obedience** and **patience** go hand in hand.

God is waiting to prove Himself a loving, caring, personal God. Are you willing to try His way? Take Him at His word—fill the **conditions** with His help, and claim Bible promises as a regular part of your daily worship. Your joy and peace will override every trial and sorrow.

Hindrance:

The opposite of the **conditions** we studied in this lesson are pretty obvious—**disobedience**, **lack of faith**, and **impatience**. Read Jeremiah 7:13,16, Proverbs 28:9 (**disobedience**), Psalm 78:58 (**unfaithfulness**), and James 1:6 (**lack of faith**). Record what God says here:

When we are **impatient**, not willing to wait upon God, and we take things into our own hands, we sin. Sin separates. Read what God says in Isaiah 59:1-2. He assures us His ear is not dull so He cannot hear. Then what does He say?

Assignment:

Continue to find promises in scripture that apply to your needs or the concerns of your family and friends, recording them on the "Record of Experiences" on page 103.

Continue to claim the promises as previously instructed. Record your answers to prayer.

Record and claim this week's **conditions** as promises asking God to help you be **obedient** and exercise **faith** and **patience**.

How did God fulfill this promise for you? Share your story:

God helped me exercise **obedience** by:

God helped me strengthen my **faith** and **patience** by:

"You can get so close to God
that nothing can hurt you."
—Mother Teresa

Derry says:
Difficult, but worth it.

Prayer of Faith Conditions: Love and Forgiveness

*For if you **forgive** men their trespasses, your heavenly Father will also **forgive** you. But if you do not **forgive** men their trespasses, neither will your Father **forgive** your trespasses.*

—Matthew 6:14-15

*Beloved, let us **love** one another, for **love** is of God; and everyone who **loves** is born of God and knows God.*

—1 John 4:7

SEVERAL YEARS AGO, I asked God to reveal any area in my life that would make Him sad and to help me see myself from His eyes. It was a very sincere prayer, but I wasn't ready for His answer. When my diagnosis came back with a second life-threatening disease, I was upset. I thought, "Lord, this isn't fair." I was angry for about an hour, then I cried—a lot. In my turmoil I remembered reading somewhere disease grows from a hotbed of resentment and bitterness. "Lord, I don't think I am burying any resentment or bitterness," I argued.

That evening I asked my family to excuse me for awhile. I went to my room with a notebook and pen and sat before the Lord. I said, "Okay Father, please dictate. If I have any resentment or bitterness buried in my heart, please reveal it. Please tell me who is involved and why." The Lord *did*; He began to dictate. There were four people on my list; one of my sons, my mother, my husband, and I can't remember whom else.

I thought I had **forgiven** them long ago, but that's not what the Lord showed me. After I thought about it, I could see how my responses to each of them had been reflecting unreleased hurt, disappointment, or feelings of rejection and betrayal. In general, each infraction actually looked relatively minor on paper. I was ashamed and disappointed—in me.

I thanked God for showing me how I looked in His eyes. I confessed the Holy Spirit was right. Sorrowfully, I repented and asked for a new heart. I had been kidding myself, but not God. He knew the secrets of my heart. Disease wasn't the main problem. I needed a "heart transplant."

I thanked God for my illness. I would much rather deal with disease than give up eternity with my Lord. God was **faithful** to fulfill His promise, *To open their eyes, and to turn them from darkness to light, and from the power of Satan unto God, that they may receive **forgiveness** of sins, and inheritance among them which are sanctified by **faith** that is in Me.*[182]

Before I closed my time with God, I asked another favor. I was saddened there were unresolved issues next to my husband's name. I was reminded of the promised command, *And above all these things put on **love**, which is the bond of perfectness,*[183] so I asked God to help me make a list of the things that were special about my husband; things I appreciated. I invited my husband in and shared with him my experience with the Lord and the notes I had taken. I told him how sorry I was that these issues had been affecting my attitude toward him, and I asked for **forgiveness**. We had prayer together and burned the list. I thought I had peace before, but it was nothing compared to how I felt after that evening! God requires us to **forgive** 70 x 7 (Matthew 18:22). If He expects that kind of a **forgiving** heart from us, how much more **forgiving** is He?

This was only the beginning. My heart-searching, surrendering, and repentance brought healing to my memories and healing to my body. Healing is not always cure but in this case there has been no further sign of disease. Our Father God is anxious for us to love each other with a pure love and forgive each other completely. The two go hand in hand. Sometimes it has been necessary for me to pray, "Father help me **love** with Your **love** and **forgive** with Your **forgiveness** because of myself, I am not able." Jesus instructs us to **love** *one another, as I have* **loved** *you.*[184]

> Father help me love with Your love and **forgive** with Your **forgiveness** because of myself, I am not able.

God's **forgiveness** so freely given is a wonderful gift. It is a release from those things that bind you. It offers peace and fills your heart with joy. On this earth we will always need the **forgiving** power of God. We are being presumptuous however if we think we can repeat the same sin over and over and keep coming back for **forgiveness**. We must cling to the text of encouragement that we are to go and *sin no more.*[185] To confess we have sinned and repent by changing our course of action are both necessary. "God wants to do more for us than **forgive** our transgressions. He is waiting for us to claim the power that will keep us from sinning."[186]

Once our sins are **forgiven**, they are no longer brought up again by our loving Father. While He may not bring them up again, we often do. We are the ones who have to "**forgive** ourselves" and stop replaying the record. We can be our own worst enemy.

"**Forgiving** oneself" is actually a contemporary expression. Nowhere in the *Bible* are we told to "**forgive** yourself." We are told, *If we confess our sins, He is faithful and just to*

151

forgive *us our sins and to cleanse us from all unrighteousness.*[187] When we don't accept His gift of **forgiveness** and think we have to **forgive** ourselves we are setting ourselves up as "over" God. Either His word is true—or not. Either He is God—or not. But *we* are not God. Sins forgiven come from Calvary's payment. This is more than God just casually excusing and forgetting. Sins cost. It cost our Savior His life. If we were to face death as a result of each transgression, we would doubtless think twice.

Jesus, during the Sermon on the Mount, taught *Therefore if you bring your gift to the altar, and there remember that your brother has something against you, leave your gift there before the altar, and go your way.*

> When we don't accept His gift of **forgiveness** and think we have to **forgive** ourselves we are setting ourselves up as "over" God.

First be reconciled to your brother, and then come and offer your gift.[188] Did you catch that? God is so serious about things being right between us, He even admonishes us to leave the altar and make sure everything is right between our brother and us. Unfortunately, we probably all have had times when we hear 'through the grapevine' someone has something against us. We may not harbor any hard feelings against them, but we learn we have in some way caused an offense. According to the above text, we have a responsibility to resolve the matter, without delay. **Love** and **forgiveness**—the two go hand in hand. *Help us, O God our Savior, for the glory of Your name; deliver us and* ***forgive*** *our sins for Your name's sake.*[189]

Before you go to sleep at night, talk it over with the person you have offended, in a spirit of humility and **love**. Scripture admonishes us to *not let the sun go down on our wrath.*[190] Consult God before you speak, requesting Divine wisdom and grace for reconciliation. *For if ye* ***forgive*** *men their trespasses, your heavenly Father will also* ***forgive*** *you: but if ye* ***forgive*** *not men their trespasses, neither will your Father* ***forgive*** *your trespasses.*[191]

It would be well for you to turn to 2 Corinthians 2:5-11. There you will find six steps for dealing with sin and **forgiveness** you might find worth studying.

"There is a grave danger in cherishing unloving thoughts, secret grievances and grudges, seemingly slight antipathies, or any hidden contempt for anyone at all."[192] Our lives are full enough of injuries, both real and imagined, given and received. As long as we continue to contemplate them and allow them to clutter our heart and mind, we are interrupting and interfering with the sweet communion the Lord would like to have with us. Jesus is a safe Place to confess our feelings. All the pain, resentment, blame, condemnation, desire to retaliate, name-calling and character judgments that could permanently damage reputations and cause irrevocable damage can all be said to an understanding Father. Our loving Father will help us sort it out.

There is some pretty strong counsel in the *Bible* about this subject. In fact we are admonished to *Let no corrupt communication proceed out of your mouth, but that which is good to the use of edifying, that it may minister grace unto the hearers. And grieve not the Holy Spirit of God, whereby ye are sealed unto the day of redemption. Let all bitterness and wrath, and anger, and clamor, and evil speaking, be put away from you, with all malice: and be ye kind one to another, tender-hearted, **forgiving** one another, even as God for Christ's sake hath **forgiven** you.*[193]

God simply requires we have the willingness to **forgive** others. If we have an unforgiving spirit it not only interferes with our relationship with men but also with God. "He who is at peace with God and his fellow men cannot be made miserable."[194] When we have a spirit of **forgiveness** toward others. we are much more open to recognize and admit our own faults. If we do not have a spirit of **forgiveness**, our *Father, which is in heaven, will not **forgive** our trespasses.*[195]

There is no limit to God's **forgiveness** toward us, therefore there should be no limit to our **forgiveness** of others. We are to *Be kind one to another, tenderhearted, **forgiving** one another, even as God for Christ's sake hath **forgiven** you.*[196]

> There is no limit to God's **forgiveness** toward us, therefore there should be no limit to our **forgiveness** of others.

The *Bible* says *fulfill ye My joy, that ye be likeminded, having the same **love**, being of one accord, of one mind. Let nothing be done through strife or vain glory: but in lowliness of mind let each esteem others better than themselves. Look not every man on his own things, but every man also on the things of others. Let this mind be in you, which was also in Christ Jesus.*[197]

If we really want to know the mind of Christ we will remember when Jesus was on the cross He said, *Father, **forgive** them for they know not what they do.* Jesus didn't spend time "chewing" on the offenses done to Him. He carried no grudges to the grave. His **love** was so great, **forgiveness** was spontaneous and complete. Why then should we not do the same?

Pray for your enemies, for those who rub you the wrong way. How often do we look at those around us and take our eyes off God. We focus on the wrong picture. At these times, God promises us grace. The lexicon definition of grace is the 'Divine influence on the heart and the reflection in our life.' If we are filled with God's character, we will **love** and accept those whom we find difficult. My mother used to say, "It's easy to **love** the lovable, but hard to **love** the unlovable. Focus on what is hard and you will be a better person." Time spent in prayer shows up on our face and in our actions. We cannot hide the outcome of our time alone with God.

If we truly want to follow Christ's example, we will take note of His instruction in Romans 12:14, *Bless those who persecute you; bless, and do not curse.*

154

I recently attended a conference that had a life-changing impact on me. It consisted of parallel themes. One was "The Unoffendable Christ." The other was, "Bless Your Enemies."

A frequent prayer of mine is, "Father, help me be more like Jesus." I don't present a list of Jesus' character qualities to God with that prayer. I simply ask to be like Jesus.

As I listened to the speaker talk about the 'Unoffendable Christ,' I thought that's how I want to be. So I prayed God would help me follow Jesus' example and live without taking offense.

Next, I listened to the speaker share how Jesus blessed those who persecuted and abused Him. I looked up the texts in the *Bible*. Sure enough, there it was in *red* letters—Jesus' words. In Luke 6:27-28 ESV *But I say to you who hear,* **Love** *your enemies, do good to those who hate you, bless those who curse you, pray for those who abuse you.*

It was King David who wanted to destroy his enemies and called upon God to punish them—get even. But Jesus blessed His enemies. I read through the text and allowed the Holy Spirit to quicken my mind to what was being taught. I prayed a heartfelt commitment to apply this instruction; these two themes to my life. This resolve was soon tested.

I had a five-hour ride home. When I finally arrived I was tired, hungry and anxious to unpack and prepare for the new week. One of my sons was home. I entered the house, greeting those present. Not having had a good day, my son greeted me with less than respect. As a matter of fact, his response was downright rude.

My unspoken thought was, "whatever is wrong with him?" Disgruntled by his greeting I carried my things into my room. As I set my suitcases down I suddenly remembered,

"The Unoffendable Christ, blessed." And David prays, *Let the words of my mouth and the meditations of my heart be acceptable in Thy sight, O Lord my strength and my Redeemer.*[198]

I went to my office and began praying. "Father, please bless my son. Please bless him with respect and honor for his parents; with the gift of desire for relationship and unity; with unconditional **love** and repentance. Please bless him with the gift of communication, a desire for reconciliation, and a cheerful spirit; with the knowledge that You are the parent Who is always there for him even when he feels his earthly parents have failed him."

It was only a few minutes later when he stormed up the office stairway to confront me. I had already applied my "secret weapon." I could not be moved. Peace prevailed and I celebrated victory. *I have been crucified with Christ, it is no longer I who live, but Christ lives in me and the life which I now live in the flesh I live by faith in the Son of God, who **loved** me and gave Himself for me.*[199]

Unfortunately there are times in our lives when we wear our feelings on our shoulder where they can easily be knocked off. Other times we have built walls of protection around our hearts so nothing will hurt us. Is that because we have been hurt so much already? Or maybe it is that we have not let go of past pain, because we have not been able to forgive. We are still bound up with all the complexities of the emotional response that first emerged. Scripture has encouragement for us, *Let the wicked forsake his way, and the unrighteous man his thoughts: and let him return unto the Lord, and He will have mercy upon him; and to our God, for He will abundantly pardon.*[200] How many have withered at our hand because we are not quick to ask for or give **forgiveness** and share our **love**?

"Who can know the depth and intensity of the heart of God? No one could measure His sorrow over an unrepentant sinner or His joy over a spiritual rebel who relinquishes everything to Him. We can begin to understand what is on the heart of God only when He shares His heart with us. (Amos 3:7) Are you aware of the fervent emotions in the soul of your Lord, as He carries the weight of the world? The disciples were unaware of the deep anguish in the heart of Jesus. Yet, He willingly shared His heart with them.

"You can choose to be alert to the heart of God. As you seek to understand what God is feeling, He may share with you the intensity of His heart. When you are around other people, God may sensitize you to the **love** He feels for them. When you see others suffering, you may feel the compassion Jesus feels. When sinners return to God in repentance, you may share the Father's joy."[201] It would delight the Father if you choose to understand His heart.

Hindrance:

The opposite of the **'Love' condition** is 'hate' or **indifference**. **Hate** can cause us to be violent or commit abominations. Study Ezekiel 8:17-18. What does God say He will not do?

Husbands—there is a text written just for you. It would be well for you to take notice. Turn to 1 Peter 3:7. What does God admonish you to do?

Wives reading this book: Caution regarding how you handle the above information. **Loving** confrontation given respectfully with thoughtful timing will be to your advantage.

The opposite of **'Forgiveness'** is **'unforgiving hear**t.' Our opening text, Matthew 6:14-15 is noteworthy. What will you do about it?

Assignment:

Record and claim this week's **conditions** as promises asking God to help you. Claim your promises daily, as you have been practicing, with your *Bible* open. Journal your answers to prayer.

Read 2 Corinthians 2:5-11. Outline the six steps for dealing with sin and **forgiveness**.

Study the following texts on **forgiveness**. Write out the texts here and on the next pages. Record how they speak to you:

• 1 John 1:9

- Romans 8:1

- Isaiah 43:25

- Jeremiah 31:34

- Psalm 19:13

- Psalm 79:9

Take two sheets of paper, pray and ask God to reveal:

- Anyone you need to **forgive**—including yourself.
- Anyone you need to ask **forgiveness** from.

List your answers. Pray over them asking God to help you address each issue. If you are struggling to **forgive**, ask God to help you **forgive** with His **forgiveness** and **love** with His **love**.

According to God's will, and being sensitive as to how your confession will affect them, confront and apologize kindly to each person on your list, if appropriate.

Ask God's **forgiveness** as well, with a humble and repentant heart.

Do you feel like you have a new lease on life? Record your experiences below. Share your stories dealing with **forgiveness** issues:

Instead of getting upset with _____, I asked God to bless them by:

This week, if you become irritated with someone, practice blessing them.

Derry says:
A small heart investment brings big
dividends.

CONCERN FOR OTHERS/INTERCESSION

If anyone sees his brother commit a sin that does not lead
to death, he should pray and God will give him life.
—1 John 5:16

IT HAD BEEN a difficult day. I was tired and ready to go home. In fact, I was looking forward to a relaxing shower. After that, my agenda was bed with a book. I needed to unwind from the day and refresh in the Lord before going to sleep.

Ready to leave work, I had just locked up my file cabinets and had grabbed my car keys when the phone rang. I looked at my watch. It was 10:30pm. I debated, then picked up the phone. "Derry, we have a patient on 2 South asking for a chaplain. We can't get this man to stop crying. We have no idea what is wrong. He has a heart condition, but death is not imminent. Can you please come see him?"

I put away my keys, picked up my *Bible*, and began praying. As I walked upstairs to Bill's room I prayed all the way; asking for wisdom, the right words and God's intervention. "Father, I prayed this morning I would put others before myself and be more **concerned** about their needs than my own; now please give me words of wisdom to help this man. Again I claim the promise in Isaiah 50:4, *that* *you will give me a tongue of the learned that I might hear and speak a word to him that is weary."*

As I entered, he looked at me in anger. (I think he was expecting a male chaplain.) He sat up, pointed his finger at me, and gruffly spit out the question, "Have you ever been in a war?"

Praying for the right answer, I said, "Sometimes I think every day of life can be like a war." He melted and began to cry. I took his hand. He said, "I don't know what to do. I was in the Korean War in 1952 and I killed a man. I haven't slept through the night since then. I have had night terrors every night. I can't go on like this. I have been to counseling, to support groups, to my priest. He told me I was forgiven and to go and sin no more. Nothing has helped. I can't live this way any longer."

While he was talking, I was praying. In my heart I thought, "Lord if he has been to all those places for help, what can I say or do? Please **help me help him**." God directed me to the *Bible* on his bedside table. I picked it up and read from 1 John 1:9, *If we confess our sins, He is faithful and just to forgive us our sins and cleanse us from all unrighteousness.* Then I said, "God's word tells us He will remove our sins *as far as the east is from the west;*[202] and *Come let us reason together, though your sins be as scarlet, they shall be white as snow.*[203] Maybe what you need to do is ask God to forgive you for not believing Him."

After we talked about that for a few minutes, he said, "Yes, that's it. I think I do. But I don't know how to pray. Will you help me?"

I told him, "Sometimes when my patients don't know how to pray, I will pray first and they will repeat after me if they agree. Would you like to do that?"

"Yes," he replied.

He closed his eyes with his hand tightly holding mine; so tight, our knuckles were white. I began to pray and then waited. He didn't repeat after me. I prayed some more and no response. I opened my eyes and looked at him. His head was pushed hard against his pillow. His lips were pressed tightly together. He was stiff and stretched out. I stopped praying and waited for his response. Nothing. I asked him if I could just **pray boldly for him**. Again he agreed.

We had already been sharing about the war in heaven, and then on earth, between Christ and Satan. It looked like the war was on in this room. I began **interceding** on his behalf. I prayed he would be released from the bondage he was under and that Jesus would set him free. I asked for the infilling of the Holy Spirit and for healing of mind, body, soul, and spirit. I felt his hand begin to relax in mine. I concluded the prayer and looked at him. His whole countenance had changed. He said, "Something has happened. I have never felt this way before." "Are you ready to pray now?" I asked. "Yes" he answered with excitement.

We both prayed. When I opened my eyes and looked at him, he was glowing. He had a smile that covered his face. "I hope I can sleep tonight," he shared.

I smiled and squeezed his hand. "You will sleep tonight. How long are you supposed to be in the hospital?"

"Four days," he reported.

"Okay, get a good night's sleep and I will check in on you sometime tomorrow."

The next day when I went into his room he was glowing. Smiling from ear to ear, he said, "I slept all night. The first time in over 50 years. Thank you, thank you."

I was thrilled for him and so grateful to our Lord and Savior. I promised to visit him again.

Later that afternoon my pager went off. I was being called to his room. As I hurried down the hallway I cried out to God. Please no, Lord. Don't take his life. He has just been healed of a lifetime of bondage.

When I walked into the room, he was sitting up in the chair putting on his shoes. His wife was all but doing a little jig around him, she was so happy. "What gives?" I asked.

"I'm going home. The doctor came in and said, "I don't know what you're doing in here. There's nothing wrong with you. You can go home.""

Praise the Lord. God did heal him body, mind, soul and spirit. Bill had been in and out of the hospital rather frequently prior to this stay, but he hasn't been back since.

What if I hadn't stayed that night? What if I hadn't answered the phone? What if I had put my own comfort or needs first? There was a time when I might have just let the phone ring. What if I didn't know how to **intercede** for others? What if I had been so self-absorbed in my own pain that I had lost my ability to think about or notice the needs of others? How could I have helped Bill that night? It is not easy to think of other people before ourselves— unless—we have made it a habit. A habit so ingrained, we don't even think twice. I'm afraid I still have more growing to do in that area. But thank God He was able to get through to me that night. I would have missed witnessing a life-changing, healing miracle.

How many lives are hurting because of our unwillingness to step out of our own shoes and stand in the shoes of others and look at things from their eyes. There are so many opportunities to take up our duty, obligation, and privilege of **intercession**, and present before our great Father God **on behalf of** those He puts in our path. We can know a lot. Our heads can be filled with volumes of information, but until we apply it, until we share it with others, it is of no value. If we don't use what we have learned, we will eventually lose it. God blesses us so we can bless others. What God gives to us we can give away in blessings or in testimony. It is not how much we do but how much love we put behind it. As we bless others, we in turn are blessed and strengthened.

Jesus is our example in all things. He prayed for His friends, for those who hated Him, and for future followers. He came to this earth to seek and save the lost, to minister to the needs of the people, to offer hope, healing, and salvation. Prayer played an important part in His daily effectiveness in reaching the needs of others. "In this work all the angels of heaven are ready to cooperate. All the resources of heaven are at the command of those who are **seeking to save** the lost."[204]

Men and women all over the world are in need of healing; physical, mental, emotional and spiritual. They are praying for divine enlightenment and intervention. We are given the opportunity to be God's hands and mouthpiece. *You are My witnesses, says the Lord, and My servants whom I have chosen; that you may know and believe Me, and understand that I am He: before Me there was no God formed, neither shall there be after Me: This people have I formed for Myself; they shall show forth My praise.*[205]

God is longing for us to work with Him, **on behalf of** His people. It is our privilege and an honor that we have been entrusted with this responsibility. He could have the angels do this work, but He has chosen to include us. *Even every one that is called by My name: for I have created him for My glory.*[206] The reward is God's presence in our life.

I recently went to an all-day seminar presented in support of "Disability Awareness Week." What concern for others was exemplified in this group. What sensitivity each had to the other disabled who were present. These dear ones have learned to appreciate life. They have excitement and gratitude for gaining success in areas many of us take for granted in our daily living and functioning. Here are people who have learned to care. Perhaps those of us who have not learned such caring are the ones who are disabled.

Our Heavenly Father knows as we impart, we grow. We grow in faith, trust, love, dependence on God, and in gratitude. Not only is it an honor to **intercede** and work with God, it is an asset.

As we depend on Him, we are reminded of Jesus' prayer recorded in John 17 **interceding** on behalf of His disciples—then and now. But one of the most unbelievable examples of **intercession** was the one He uttered on the cross, *Father, forgive them for they know not what they do.*[207]

God wants us to be concerned about others and to care enough that we will be **intercessors**. We need perceptive spirits that notice when others are shriveling up before our eyes. Even the strongest Christian can be beaten down when ignored and when those around fail to offer 'nourishment.' How often do we use the wrong approach? If only we would realize how much God desires for us to take advantage of every opportunity to encourage a burdened soul, to offer the hope of a risen Savior and of a loving Father. Each of us needs to ask God to help us be aware of those around us in need of a ray of our sunshine. We are of little value to God in this work if we are dependent upon our own wisdom and choices. How can we be effective for God in our ministry to others if we are unwilling to invest time in others and **intercede** for them in prayer?

> We cannot hold onto negative feelings about the people we are praying for, for very long.

To the best of our ability we need to make sure there are no impediments in our relationships with other people if we want to be effective **intercessors**. We need cleansed hearts and minds for the labor of **intercession**. If we have done all we can to heal broken relationships and issues are still not reconciled, Jesus considers our attempts and the honesty of our heart. We cannot hold onto negative feelings about the people we are praying for, for very long.

Once we start praying, we recognize we now have a vested interest. Our adverse feelings become swallowed up in an earnest desire for the salvation of the one for whom we are **interceding**. To a heart that loves, **intercession** is a privileged necessity. There can be nothing between ourselves and our Savior.

In our **intercession** we may see little or no results,

> The deeper our surrender to God, the more true and powerful will be our **intercession**.

but we are to continue in our prayers. We will find this perseverance will bring heart changes also in us and enables God's perfect love to flow from an imperfect 'us.' "The deeper our surrender to God, the more true and powerful will be our **intercession**."[208]

It is God Who speaks to our hearts and urges us to pray for those He brings to our mind. If our hearts were truly open to pray for others, we would be softened and melted by Jesus' love. We would watch and wait to see the blessings of God poured out in behalf of those we **intercede** for. Rejoicing would fill our hearts as we see God's hand active in their lives. Instead of selfishly concentrating on our own needs or desires, unselfish love would remind us to put others before the throne of grace, carrying their problems to God for solutions.

Preparation in working for and with others begins with prayer. Why would we even consider moving forward without having first spent time in surrendered heartfelt petition? Isn't it amazing we would even consider 'doing' for the Savior—without the Savior? **Intercession** comes from a heart of love. **Intercession** is love in action.

The greatest gift we can give is a listening ear, an accepting heart, and a commitment to **intercede** to our all-caring God who will hear and act in their best interest. We are drawn to **intercede** by the love God has planted in our hearts. As we pray, we must pray for the will of God on behalf of those we are praying for. The love of God will flow through us and use us to bless His people. Pray, *"Here am I, send me. I'm available, Lord."*

When Job realized the lifestyle of his children was not in accordance to God's will, he prayed for them. He asked God to forgive them, and he offered burnt offerings on their behalf.

They were adults living on their own. There was little Job could do for them now, but he did what he could. He prayed and offered sacrifices.

By his example we are invited to be active when concerns for friends and loved ones burden our hearts. We are to do what we can. We may be stopped from doing any obvious deed, but no one can interfere with, or keep us from offering prayers on their behalf.

Continual, consistent, sincere prayer on behalf of the oppressed can come only from a heart of love. Moses exemplified the epitome of love when he **interceded** for the rebellious Israelites. He told God *But now, if you will, forgive their sin—and if not, please blot me out from Your book which you have written*[209] What love! It is beyond my comprehension that one could love so much, he would sacrifice eternity with our God for the sake of others.

Someone once said, "When we see our Lord coming, there is only one regret we might have—that we have not taken the time to **intercede** and minister on behalf of those whom God has given us." "Do you feel that it is too great a sacrifice to yield all to Christ? Ask yourself the question "What has Christ given for me?"[210] "The blessing comes when, by faith, the soul surrenders itself to God."[211] He needs us all in His service. The highest calling is to save souls for the Kingdom.

My prayer for us is: Soften our hearts Lord Jesus, and help us to die of our selfishness and lack of concern for

those suffering around us. Help us invest in the investment that pays the greatest dividend by spending time on
our knees, **interceding** on behalf of Your children, and
action in reaching out as we listen and follow Your divine
instructions. One day may You say to us, *Well done, good
and faithful servant; Thou hast been faithful over a few
things, I will make thee ruler over many things: enter thou
into the joy of thy Lord.*—Matthew 25:23 KJV.

Hindrance:

The opposite of "**Concern for Others** and **Intercession**" is
"**Selfish Motives**." Look up James 4:3, and complete the
following verse: "Ye ask and receive ..."

Another hindrance is found in Proverbs 21:13, "**neglect of
mercy**." Record it here:

Assignment:

Record and claim this week's conditions as promises asking God to help you. Claim your promises daily, as you have been practicing, with your *Bible* open. Journal your answers to prayer.

Now that you have learned all the conditions, be sure you commit them to memory. When you pray, you can say, "Father, please help me fulfill all the conditions to answered prayer so I do not become presumptuous or offend You."

Since you now have them memorized, just review them monthly so they remain fresh in your mind and you don't become slothful.

Start a list of people you would like to **intercede** for and their specific needs. Ask God if there is someone He wants you to be **praying for**. Listen. Names will come to your mind.

Find Bible promises appropriate for their needs and pray over them, also claiming the promise in 1 John 5:16.

Now is the time to use your new "Prayer Journal" to keep track of those you are **praying for** and the answers. Watch for answers to your prayers.

Are there any areas in your life where selfishness is keeping you from being effective for God? List these and commit them to God.

Share your story:

God answered my **prayer on behalf of** _____ by:

"Prayer becomes a sacrificial offering of ourselves
to God, to become agents of God's presence and
action in the daily events and situations of our lives."
—M. Robert Mulholland, Jr.,
Invitation to a Journey

Summary

Derry says:
Look how far you've come!

Perfecting Private Prayer

Therefore I will look to the LORD; I will wait for the God of
my salvation; My God will hear me.
                —Micah 7:7

GOSPEL PRINCIPLES OF CONDITIONS to claiming God's promises:

- Commands are promises—John 15:7

- Victory through surrender to God's will—John. 15:5

- Cooperate with God—Mark 9:24

- God backs every promise—Numbers 23:19

- Through promises we become partakers of the divine nature—2 Peter 1:3,4

- Promises are conditional—Jeremiah 18:1-11

- No power of self to fulfill conditions—Jeremiah 13:23

- Promises are available and plentiful—2 Corinthians 7:1

Conditions upon which we may expect God will hear and answer our prayers:

Verbal Conditions

- Ask—Matthew 7:7-8
- Believe—Mark 11:24
- Give Thanks—Philippians 4:6

General Conditions

- Need of God—Mark 2:17
- Ask in Jesus Name—John 14:13,14
- Perseverance—Ephesians 6:18
- Diligence (carefulness, steady application)—Hebrews 12:15
- Seek First Kingdom of God—Matthew 6:31-33
- Responsive heart—2 Kings 22:19
- Humility, Repentance—2 Kings 22:19
- Obedience—1 John 3:21-22
- Faith—Hebrews 11:6
- Patience—Hebrews 6:12
- Love—1 John 4:7
- Forgiveness—Matthews 6:14-15
- Concern for others—Ephesians 6:18, 1 John 5:16
- Pure heart—Psalm 66:18

Hindrances to Answered Prayers:

- Reject God—1 Samuel 8:18
- Unfaithful—Psalm 78:57,58
- Instability—James 1:6-8
- Seek other gods—Jeremiah 11:13-14
- Rebellious—Deuteronomy 1:43, 45
- Arrogance—Job 35:12-13 NIV
- Disobedience—Jeremiah 7:13,16, Proverbs 28:9
- Lack of Faith—James 1:6
- Impatient—Isaiah 59:1,2
- Hate—Ezekiel 8:17,18
- Unforgiving heart—Matthew 6:14, 15
- Selfish motives—James 4:3
- Neglect of mercy—Proverbs 21:13
- Cherished sins—Psalm 66:18

Important Hindrance for Married Couples:

- Dishonoring to spouse—1 Peter 3:7

"The extent of your faith and trust in the promises of God has a definite effect upon your attitudes and thinking. Such things as tension, anxiety, and emotional stress, as well as many instances of physical and spiritual disintegration, result from a lack of inner harmony and peace of mind."
—Dr. Hobart Freeman,
Positive Thinking & Confession

Part Four

"With God being full of both wisdom and love,
why not constantly turn to Him for guidance
and counsel, enjoying always the blessing of
His matchless leadership and loving care?"
—Edwin R. Thiele,
Knowing God

Derry says:
I'd rather walk in the will of God
than demand my own way.

PRAYER OF COMMITMENT

Nevertheless not my will but Thine be done.
—Luke 22:42

WHEN I WAS a new Christian, I had not yet learned how to pray the Prayer of **Commitment**, the "If it is Thy will" prayer. My husband had been out of work for some time with a concussion. We were then on the verge of losing our new home we had worked and saved so hard to buy. I had a terrible problem with worry in those days, and the whole situation seemed overwhelming to me. I would cry for hours as I contemplated the future. We had two little boys to care for and there was no money coming in. If we lost our home, or even sold it, where could we move that we could even afford? The future seemed so bleak and uninviting. I didn't understand all my foreboding could be set free with just a moment of genuine praying. Asking God to do '**according to His will**,' would have saved so many tears.

God was persevering with me. One day as I was lying on my bed sobbing my heart out, it was as though I heard God say, "Derry, why are you crying? You don't even know the outcome yet. If things do not work out as you hope they will, then you deserve a good cry. But if everything works out well, look at all the time you have wasted. Stop crying, watch, and wait." While those might not have been His exact words, the message was the same.

This experience changed my life. It was as though a light-bulb went off in my head. I realized how foolish I had been. From then on I have been relatively free of worry. Waiting can be trying, but when you know your Father loves you, you are assured He will only allow what is ultimately best for you and yours.

There are times we will have specific requests but there will be no promise to reveal God's will. That is the time we pray the **Prayer of Commitment**. We pray the Prayer of Faith/Prayer of Reception when we already know God's will because it is specifically stated in the promise. But even when a promise is specific, there are times we should couple our Prayer of Reception with the **Prayer of Commitment**. Examples of this might be when we are considering a move, need a home, choosing a college or life work, hoping for a companion, or facing health issues and decisions.

One of the most frequently discussed **Prayer of Commitment** centers around health and healing. I remember when my husband's diagnosis came back—cancer. After three surgeries it was very hard to want to "commit" to God's will. We weren't ready to consider life without a husband and a father. When are any of us ever ready to part with someone we love? Often we have no warning.

It is difficult to go forward with a surrendered heart when you are in fear of a dear one dying, or if you are facing severe health problems yourself. But the enemy uses fear to keep us off balance. God wants us to face our fear squarely. This we can do by letting go and giving control, permission, acceptance to God's will. God knows the end from the beginning.

When we are praying for the sick we are instructed to do our part, knowing the ultimate decision for healing is up to God. Life and healing come from the Father.

As we study God's word, it is clear His desire is to heal. Scripture is filled with healing promises. In fact in Matthew 10:7-8 we are commissioned to go preach, heal, raise the dead, cast out devils. We really need no other evidence to support the truth that it is not God's desire for His children to suffer illness.

This leaves us somewhat perplexed. Many of us have fasted and agonized in persevering prayer, with total obedience and submission for the healing of one we care about—but to no avail. If the promises are true, how can we accept or explain this? We may have questioned our faith or the faith of the one we have prayed for. None of it makes sense to us. We wonder where God is.

Although there are many healing promises in the *Bible*, we need to consider God's foreknowledge regarding each of us. Would healing and longer life cause us to lose our eternal life because we might turn away from God? Only He knows. He is desirous of us all spending eternity in heaven, therefore it is not wise for us to beg or plead on behalf of life without a willingness to accept God's answer. So here, we are both claiming God's promises—the Prayer of Reception and in submission to God's foreknowledge, praying the **Prayer of Commitment**.

There are those who would argue that praying with this perspective expresses a lack of faith and offers an excuse for God if healing isn't extended.

There is no question God did not create us to die. He created us for life. That plan was interrupted in the Garden of Eden. Jesus died on the cross not only to forgive us from sin, but to heal our diseases. The scripture says, *by His stripes we are healed;*[212] *He took up our infirmities and carried our diseases.*[213]*and if anyone be in Christ, he is a new creation. He makes all things new.*

During a crisis it is natural to turn to God; but consider how sad it would be if Jesus' healing enabled the one healed to return to a sinful life that would cause them to suffer the ultimate death. It is sometimes difficult for us to accept there are some who request healing with no intention of making changes in their life that would show respect for the gift given them. It is presumptuous of us to ask for healing if we have not obeyed God's laws of health nor have any intention of doing so if we are healed. If we have not respected our body as the temple of God, we are dishonoring God. Our approach should be to come before God in humility and contrition, asking God to forgive us and cleanse us.

"It is the privilege of all who comply with the conditions to know for themselves that pardon is freely extended for every sin. Put away the suspicion that God's promises are not meant for you. They are for every repentant transgressor."[214] God is always ready to forgive; but forgiving does not necessarily mean the consequences of our sins will be removed. Our Father knows whether or not we would continue in the same neglectful habits. That is why, when I pray and claim promises for healing, I ask God to, "heal and intervene for the sake of their eternal salvation, that Your plan and purposes for their life will be fulfilled and the enemy's plans thwarted."

I spoke to a gentleman at the hospital today. He was there to visit our mutual friend who has received a prognosis of two weeks' life expectancy. As we shared our tears and concerns together, he mentioned the questions he has for God: questions still unanswered regarding the death of his young son from a crippling disease. Losing people we love often leaves us with questions, and sometimes anger.

You will find God loves you so much, He can deal with your temporary anger at Him for not answering prayers according to your expectations. He loves you so much, He will look at the 'big' picture and answer accordingly.

When we do not know God's will, this as never before is the time to reach toward heaven and give Him our hand. By doing so, we are letting go and letting God. This is commitment. This is faith in action. This is praying, "Not my will but Thine be done." Not a prayer to change His mind, but to walk in conjunction with His divine plan.

When we do not know God's will, this as never before is the time to reach toward heaven and give Him our hand.

When we maintain an active, ongoing prayer life, we develop confidence in God. We learn how much He loves us, and knowing Him as our personal God, Savior, and Friend enriches our life with ongoing answers to our prayers. We find life is more bearable when we surrender control to our Lord, and when we ask for His advice as we face decisions and everyday perplexities and disappointments.

Because it is the heart of God to save His people for eternity, we can trust His judgment as to who shall sleep, and who shall remain to face the terrible days prior to His return. He knows who can stand firm and survive the trials ahead. *The righteous perish, and no one ponders it in his heart; devout men are taken away, and no one understands that the righteous are taken away to be spared from evil. Those who walk uprightly enter into peace; they find rest as they lie in for the death.*[215] That is why our Savior prayed, and it is applicable for us today especially when asking for the gift of healing, *Nevertheless, not My will, but Thine, be done.*[216]

Assignment:

Prayerfully contemplate the following questions:

What areas in your life need to be addressed "according to God's will?"

Who in your life needs healing? List them in your journal.

Contemplate: Are these persons willing to make the necessary lifestyle changes to honor their body temple and work in conjunction with God? Have they asked forgiveness for their sins and forgiven others and themselves?

How could healing in this situation glorify God?

Derry says:
Feel how much closer you've come
to Jesus.

Spiritual Warfare

*Ye are complete in Him, which is the head of all principality and power ... and having spoiled principalities and powers, He made a show of them openly, **triumphing** over them in it.*

—Colossians 2:10,15 KJV

I REMEMBER WHEN I first came back to God over 40 years ago. I had determined I would get up and have time in my *Bible* every morning before everyone else awakened. I snuggled into my little corner, wrapped up in my blanket, and began to read. I had not yet learned the necessity of prayer before reading scripture, asking the Holy Spirit to be my Teacher and illuminate my mind as I studied and claimed promises. What I read that morning, and how it impressed my emotions, caught me off guard. In scripture I was reminded of my sins, and it appeared by my reading God would have nothing to do with me, that my sins kept me from Him. I felt I would never know God, that my sins would always be remembered, that no forgiveness was available for me, and there was no hope.

I remember the desperation I felt after that time of study. Finally, I could bear it no more. I called my pastor, just to find he was out of town. I called Bible scholars—no answer. After almost a day of being tormented, thinking God no longer wanted me, I called the pastor in the next town and he agreed to come over. After I explained my fears, he warned me of Satan's cunning tactics. He reminded me the devil is well versed in Bible teachings, and is very capable of conducting a misleading study. He left me with the encouraging scripture promise that says, *Ye are complete in Him, which is the head of all principality and power, and having spoiled principalities and powers, He made a show of them openly,* **triumphing** *over them in it.*[217] He also left me with the instructions to never open my *Bible* without first asking the Holy Spirit to be my Teacher and Guide.

I don't think the archenemy gets too upset when we talk about prayer. I think he becomes riled when we actually start praying. If he keeps us so busy we don't have time to spend with God or causes us to be emotionally off balance, he's gained the upper hand. It is the plan of the enemy to cause us to sin, crush us with guilt, then leave us to believe we are beyond God's saving graces. Satan trembles when we pray. He covers his ears when we mention Jesus' name. He flees when we begin to praise.

The war between God and Satan is real. I plan to be on the winning side using prayer, praise, God's word, and the name of our victorious Jesus as my most effective weapons. Frequently during this battle we must keep in close communication with our Leader, our Commander—God. We must come to Him with a committed, open heart, asking Him to reveal weaknesses and expose vulnerable areas, spotlighting our cherished sins so we can partner with Him to overcome. Although Satan is a conquered foe, he desires to thwart our prayers.

The *Bible* teaches, *We are to wrestle against the principalities, against the powers, against the world rulers of this darkness, against the spiritual hosts of wickedness in heavenly places.*[218] We are to wrestle in prayer against Satan and his forces. Our greatest **weapon** against the enemy is prayer—deep, earnest, heartfelt, persevering, prayer and following Jesus' example by using the **sword** *of* *the Spirit*[219]—the word of God. We are to cover ourselves with the **armor** of God.

"If Satan sees that he is in danger of losing one soul, he will exert himself to the utmost to keep that one. And when the individual is aroused to his danger with distress, fervor, and, looks to Jesus for strength, Satan fears he will lose a captive and he calls a reinforcement of his angels to hedge in the poor soul, and form a wall of darkness around him, that heaven's light may not reach him.

"But if the one in danger perseveres, and in his helplessness cast himself upon the merits of the blood of Christ, our Savior listens to the earnest prayer of faith, and sends a reinforcement of those angels that excel in strength to deliver him."[220]

Many years ago my brother got mixed up with drugs. He was using the hard stuff. Every five or ten minutes he would call me and tell me how he was being followed and how we were being invaded. I was busy with six children then, and besides being totally brokenhearted and unnerved by my brother's continual calls for help, I was about at my wit's end trying to be patient with the interruptions day after day, and night after night into all hours.

I called a dedicated pastor who had known my brother when he was in school. We set up an appointment to meet and intercede. I fasted, prayed and did a lot of soul-searching and confessing for three days before our appointment. When we met, we went into prayer for him for over two hours. Every request for cleansing and healing of the evil that had penetrated his life was followed by claiming a Bible promise for **victory** in that area.

I returned home. Two days later my brother called. The minute I heard His voice I began to pray. I claimed him for our Savior, and I commanded in the name of Jesus for the enemy to leave him alone. Within the week we received another call from my brother. He was healed!!! Delivered!!!

189

He called to tell us he was off the street, living at a mission, and had a job. He was anxious to get paid and save up some money so he could get a place and begin his life over.

God's promises are sure. *And the God of Peace shall bruise Satan under your feet shortly. The grace of our Lord Jesus Christ be with you.*[221] He was true to His word. Holy Lord, most Holy Lord! You alone are worthy to be praised!

Songs of praise that speak of Jesus' name and our love for Him are also weapons we can always use against the wiles of the enemy. Satan tries to get us to stop praying and praising. He whispers in our ear that we don't deserve anything; that we are not worthy. He is right. We are not worthy of ourselves, but through Jesus, covered by His robe of righteousness we are. We are children of the King—royalty. Jesus is worthy. When we pray in Jesus name, and when we praise, the windows of heaven are opened.

Jesus was in the wilderness weak and hungry, agonizing in prayer. Satan tried three times to tempt Him, but Jesus came out victorious. After Satan's attempts to defeat Jesus, angels came and ministered to Jesus needs. Angels will encircle us and care for us as well.

"Christ is our example. Are the ministers of Christ tempted and fiercely buffeted by Satan? So also was He who knew no sin. He turned to His Father in these hours of distress. He came to earth that He might provide a way whereby we could find grace and strength to help in every time of need, by following His example in frequent, earnest prayer. If the ministers of Christ will imitate this pattern, they will be imbued with His Spirit, and angels will minister unto them."[222]

Assignment:

Have you been living in the bondage of believing Satan's lies about you? In what way?

Are you struggling to be released from restraints in your life? What are they?

Ask God to bind Satan's power over you or those you are interceding for. For suggested prayer content, see Appendix C. Modify the prayers to fit your own circumstances.

Claim the promise in Ephesians 6:10-18, that God will cover you with the **Armor of God**.

Claim the promise in John 8:36, that if *the Son shall set you free, you shall be free indeed.*

Share your story. How God set me free:

"Whenever there is prayer, there is danger
[to Satan] of His [God's] own immediate action."
—C.S. Lewis,
The Screwtape Letters

Derry says:
Don't rely on willpower when you
have God's power.

HINDRANCE TO ANSWERED PRAYER: CHERISHED SIN

*If I regard **iniquity** in my heart, The Lord will not hear me.*
—Psalm 66:18 KJV

WE HAVE SPENT a great deal of attention accentuating the conditions to answered prayers. At the close of each section an opposite 'hindrance' was included for your study. This particular 'hindrance' is being highlighted because it severely corrupts us from within—from the very core of our being if we don't acknowledge it.

God gives the specific instruction, *If I regard **iniquity** in my heart, the Lord will not hear me.*[223] Does that actually mean what it says, if we harbor secret sin in our life, God will not hear us? Renunciation is the willingness to give up our secret sins, to let go of them, and is a condition to answered prayer. This text points out that **secret sin** is a hindrance to having our prayers answered. Truly we do not want to hold onto anything that would come between God and us. As you present this command to God, ask that He will reveal anything hidden in your heart you have been unable to see.

When this truth was first taught to me, over 40 years ago; I was a choc-o-holic. You understand what that means, don't you? That means I loved chocolate. In fact, I loved chocolate so much, I drove 30 minutes to buy a five-pound box of See's candy. By the time I got home, it was almost gone. The rest I would hide around the house for my next "fix." No question, I had it pretty bad.

Is eating a piece of chocolate a sin? That's not what I'm saying. Anything in excess is. Addiction is! I was addicted. This was a **secret sin**, and I had to ask Jesus for help.

At that same time, when this truth first came into my life, I'm ashamed to have to admit I had another very embarrassing addiction—watching soap operas. I used to plan doctor appointments for the children and my grocery shopping all around getting back in time so I didn't miss one day of the programs. The happenings of those people had become part of my life. I had to ask God to help me let go of that. I had to be open to change in my life.

Our Father expects us to come to Him and confess our sins, make things right, before asking for any needs to be met. We should plead for purity of soul. God promises us *a new heart also will I give you, and a new spirit will I put within you: and I will take away the stony heart out of your flesh, and I will give you a heart of flesh. And I will put my Spirit within you, and cause you to walk in My statutes, and ye shall keep My judgments, and do them.*[224]

One **sin**, allowed to be **cherished** in our life, will rob us of God's anointing spirit and blessing. *If we say that we have no sin, we deceive ourselves, and the truth is not in us.*[225] Sin not only removes us from prayer's power but renders us useless and steals away our joy, unless we confess our sins, for *He is faithful and just to forgive us our sins and cleanse us from all unrighteousness.*[226]

Are we to believe we must be without sin in order for God to hear us? No. God is anxious for us to confess our faults and ask for forgiveness. He is also anxious that we make a complete surrender of anything in our life that would come between Him and us. Our Father loves us and wants to shower us with blessings. That means we are to relinquish any **hidden sins.** We are to have nothing between us and our Savior—not chocolate, soap operas, addictions, wrong attitudes, or anything else. It should be Jesus first, remembering He was crucified for others as well as for us.

If we **cherish sin** in our heart, we are assured God will not answer. *He who turns away his ear from hearing the law, even his prayer is an abomination.*[227] That is a pretty strong word—abomination. How does it make you feel to think because you are holding on to some known sin, God has turned away from you and is insulted by your communication to Him? Obedience is better than presumption. It is possible if we are not willing to obey and surrender, but instead hang on tenaciously to our **prized sin,** that if we do get answers, they won't be from God. Remember, Satan is coming as an angel of light and will be happy to deceive us into a self-complacent prayer life that lacks obedience.

Do you remember the story of David? He committed adultery and then had the innocent husband, his faithful commander, put to death. David had to suffer the results of his sin. There were consequences. God did indeed punish David, but He forgave Him. If there was restoration for David, there is hope for us.

We might think we aren't so bad, but as we allow
God's searchlight into our hearts we may be sadly surprised. As we see ourselves from His eyes, with a receptive spirit, we will see that changes need to be made. As we contemplate His character and the gift of salvation so freely offered from His sacrifice, we will be moved to tears of shame. To think our ingratitude would cause us to put anything or anyone before our Lord is disconcerting. If we are unwilling to obey God, why should we expect Him to answer our petitions?

> If we are unwilling to obey God, why should we expect Him to answer our petitions?

197

Assignment:

I realize now I have **cherished sin** in my life. I will confess this before God and relinquish:

Claim a promise for the opposite of your **cherished sin** and list it on the "Record of Experiences" on page 103. Prayerfully review the next several pages on "Hindrances to Answered Prayer," asking God to reveal any areas in your life needing adjustment.

With God's help I will overcome my **cherished sin** by:

HINDRANCES TO ANSWERED PRAYER

"Wherever there is something in our life that is not conformed to the image of Christ, there is a place where we are incapable of being all that God wants us to be to others ... restricted in its effectiveness and fullness ..."
—M. Robert Mulholland, Jr.,
Invitation to a Journey

THE FOLLOWING IS A LIST of scriptures where God specifically says **He will not listen to our prayers**. Please understand I have included these as warnings. If you find yourself convicted of anything on the list, go before God in repentance. These promises are not to cause you to lose hope, but to direct you and encourage you as to what changes you may need to make in your life in order to assure the Lord *will* listen. God wants us in right relationship with Him. He is anxious to forgive and help you start afresh. Having everything right between you and Him is what Jesus' victory on the cross was to accomplish.

- Numbers 12:2,8-9 KJV **Speaking against the Lord's chosen leaders**: *And they said, Hath the Lord indeed spoken only by Moses? Hath he not spoken also by us? And the Lord heard it. Why then were you not afraid to speak against my servant Moses. So the angel of the Lord banned against them and He departed.*

- Deuteronomy 1:32,45 NASB **Rebellion**: *But for all this, you did not trust the Lord your God who goes before you on your way. Then you returned and wept before the Lord, but the Lord did not listen to your voice or give ear to you.*

- 1 Samuel 8:18-19 NASB **Insist on own way**: *Then you will cry out in that day because of your king whom you have chosen for yourselves; and the Lord will not answer you in that day. Nevertheless the people refused to listen ....*

- 1 Samuel 28:6 KJV **Disobedient to God. Trust in mediums/spiritualism**: *And when Saul inquired of the Lord, the Lord answered him not.*

- Job 35:13 KJV **Vanity**: *Surely God will not hear vanity, neither will the Almighty regard it.*

- Psalm 66:18 **Secret sin cherished in heart**: *If I regard iniquity in my heart, the Lord will not hear me.*

- Psalm 78:56-59 KJV **Unfaithfulness—Other gods**: *Yet they tempted and provoked the most high God, and kept not His testimonies. But turned back, and dealt unfaithfully ... provoked Him to anger with their high places, and moved Him to jealousy with their graven images. When God heard this, he was wroth, and greatly abhorred Israel.*

- Proverbs 1:28 KJV **Disregard for God and His counsel, Indifference**: *Then shall they call upon me, but I will not answer: they shall seek me early, but they shall not find me.*

- Proverbs 21:13 KJV **No mercy**: *Whoso stoppeth his ears at the cry of the poor, he also shall cry himself, but shall not be heard.*

- Proverbs 28:9 KJV **Not obedient to God's law**: *He that turneth away his ear from hearing the law, even his prayer shall be abomination.*

- Isaiah 1:15 KJV **Murder**: *And when ye spread forth your hands, I will hide Mine Eyes from you: yea, when ye make many prayers, I will not hear: your hands are full of blood.*

- Isaiah 58:4 KJV **Wrong fasting**: *Behold, ye fast for strife and debate, and to smite with the fist of wickedness: ye shall not fast as ye do this day, to make your voice to be heard on high.*

- Isaiah 59:2 KJV **Secret sin cherished in heart**: *But your iniquities have separated between you and your God, and your sins have hid his face from you, that he will not hear.*

- Jeremiah 7:13,16 KJV **Will not listen to God or obey**: *And now, because ye have done all these works, saith the Lord, and I spake unto you, rising up early and speaking, but ye heard not; and I called you, but you answered not; ... Therefore pray not thou for this people, neither lift up cry nor prayer for them, neither make intercession to me: for I will not hear thee.*

- Jeremiah 11:3, 14 **Broken covenant, disobedience, evil hearts, and other gods**: *Thus says the Lord God of Israel: "Cursed is the man who does not obey the words of this covenant which I commanded ... So do not pray for this people, or lift up a cry or prayer for them; for I will not hear them in the time that they cry out to Me because of their trouble."*

- Ezekiel 8:17-18 KJV **Abominations, violence, anger**: *... Is it a light thing to the house of Judah that they commit the abominations which they commit here? For they have filled the land with violence, and have returned to provoke me to anger: and, lo, they put the branch to their nose. Therefore will I also deal in fury Mine Eye shall not spare, neither will I have pity: and though they cry in Mine Ears with a loud voice, yet will I not hear them.*

- Micah 3:4 KJV **Evil, murder**: *Then shall they cry unto the Lord, but he will not hear them: He will even hide His face from them at that time, as they have behaved themselves ill in all their doings.*

- Nahum 1:3, 2:13 **Guilty and unrepentant:** *The Lord is slow to anger, and great in power, and will not at all acquit the wicked ... Behold, I am against thee, saith the Lord of hosts.*

- Zechariah 7:13 KJV **No mercy**: *Therefore it is come to pass, that as he cried, and they would not hear, so they cried, and I would not hear, saith the Lord of hosts:*

- Matthew 5:21-22 KJV **Name calling, anger, murder**: *Ye have heard that it was said by them of old time, Thou shalt not kill; and whosoever shall kill shall be in danger of the judgment: But I say unto you, That whosoever is angry with his brother without a cause shall be in danger of the judgment: and whosoever shall say to his brother, Raca, shall be in danger of the council: but whosoever shall say, Thou fool, shall be in danger of hell fire.*

- Mark 11:26 **Will not forgive others or self**: *But if ye do not forgive, neither will your Father which is in heaven forgive your trespasses.*

- Luke 14:11 KJV **Self-exaltation**: *For whosoever exalteth himself shall be abased; and he that humbleth himself shall be exalted.* and James 1:6-7 KJV *... like a wave of the sea driven with the wind and tossed. For let not that man think that he shall receive any thing of the Lord.*

- James 4:3 KJV **Selfish motives**: *Ye ask, and receive not, because ye ask amiss, that ye may consume it upon your lusts.*

- 1 Peter 3:7 KJV **Husbands dishonoring to wife**: *Likewise, ye husbands, dwell with them according to knowledge, giving honor unto the wife, as unto the weaker vessel, and as being heirs together of the grace of life; that your prayers be not hindered.*

"Prayer is the act by which the people of God
become incorporated into the presence and
action of God in the world."
—M. Robert Mulholland, Jr.,
Invitation to a Journey

PART FIVE

"We live as spiritual paupers when unlimited
resources are placed at our disposal ... There's a
great difference between sitting on our problems
and standing on the promises!"
—John Ogilvie,
Devotions for Daily Reading

Derry says:
Growth is gradual. Some things
take time. Expect great things.

MY CHALLENGE TO YOU

In your relationships with one another, have the same mindset as Christ Jesus: Who, being in very nature God, did not consider equality with God something to be used to His own advantage; rather He made Himself nothing, taking the very nature of a servant, being made in human likeness. And being found in appearance as a man, He humbled Himself by becoming obedient to death—even death on a cross! Therefore God exalted Him to the highest place and gave Him the name that is above every name, that at the name of Jesus every knee should bow, in heaven and on earth and under the earth, and every tongue acknowledge that Jesus Christ is Lord, to the glory of God the Father.
—Philippians 2:5-11 NIV

ABOUT 18 YEARS AGO I was on a camping trip with my family. I awoke to a beautiful morning. I lay in my sleeping bag listening to the quiet breathing of my loved ones around me and the songs of birds worshipping God at the break of day. God often seems especially close when you are closed in by His creation; nature all around you. I began to worship God in my heart; praising and thanking Him. After some time, I desired to do some Bible reading and promise claiming. When I claim promises from scripture, I turn the pages of the *Bible* frequently.

Turning pages in a silent environment can suddenly sound very loud as the paper crackles. I feared I would wake up my family. If they woke up, excitement about the day would cause chatter to ensue. This sacred time with God would be interrupted.

I decided the best answer would be to review Bible promises I could remember and begin claiming them in my mind. After about 10 minutes of this, I began to question what I was doing for the first time. I said, "Father, do I have myself in some kind of habit that has become rote and routine? Am I honoring You or disappointing You by doing this promise-claiming, some of the same ones, day after day? Is this really what You want me to be doing?"

I lay there waiting for an answer. Then God answered me in a way He had not answered before. In my mind's eye I visualized myself in the middle of a large body of water—maybe an ocean. I was holding onto a life raft with each hand. One was in front of me and one was behind me. Then for just a moment, I released my grip on the life raft behind me. That was all it took. I could not retrieve it. It slipped further and further behind until it was no longer in view. I felt like the Lord had said, "I need you to intercede for my people. Without intercession, they may be lost forever. These promises are for you and for those I give you. Be faithful."

My challenge to you is inspired from the above story. You know people I will never meet; people God has given you. The way you reflect Christ to others, and your faithfulness in interceding for them, may make the difference in their eternal salvation—and yours as well. "There are many who need the ministration of loving Christian hearts. Many have gone down to ruin who might have been saved if their neighbors, common men and women, had put forth personal effort for them. Many are waiting to be personally addressed. The saving and sanctifying truth cannot be shut up in our heart.

"All who are consecrated to God will be channels of light. God makes them His agents to communicate to others the riches of His grace ... One of the most effective ways of winning souls to Him is in exemplifying His character in our daily life ... But **in order for us to develop a character like Christ's we must share in His work**. In order to enter into His joy, the joy of seeing souls redeemed by His sacrifice, we must participate in His labors for their redemption."[228] Sharing what has been imparted helps us continue to grow.

Will you be faithful in applying the word of God, and receive the power from His word, to claim the fullness of life for yourself and those whom God is entrusting to you? If so, I pray you will sign the following covenant, trusting God to help you fulfill all you desire to be for Him. I encourage you to continue to apply what you have learned and commit to pray *in the "YES" of God* and then study deeper *Growing in the "Yes" of God*.

If you have not yet committed to following Christ, I invite you to turn back to page xx and pray the "Prayer of Surrender."

Closing Prayer

In the name of Jesus, and by the power vested by Him, I commit to live my life to honor my Lord. I will follow my Lord's example and become familiar with scripture, presenting the commands and promises to God for fulfillment as I work in partnership with Him to love and influence souls for the glory of the Kingdom.

Signed this _____ day of _____, 20___.

_____

Signature

FINAL THOUGHTS

*And I heard a loud voice from heaven saying, "Behold, the
tabernacle of God is with men, and He will dwell with them,
and they shall be His people. God Himself will be with them
and be their God. And God will wipe away every tear from
their eyes; there shall be no more death, nor sorrow, nor
crying. There shall be no more pain, for the former things
have passed away ... Behold, I make all things new ...
Write, for these words are true and faithful.*
　　　　　　　　　　—Revelation 21:3-5

JUST LISTEN TO THE NEWS. Compare it with the pro-
phetic words of scripture and you will find that truly
Jesus is coming soon. To make it through the time
ahead, before His return, we must know His promises and
the power of His word.

I can't say it enough: our Father, our Jesus and our Holy
Spirit want to have a personal relationship with each of
us. Relationships take work. They take communication
and continuity. The only way we will ever "feel" close to
our Lord is to spend time with Him. Someone once said,
"God wants to control our mind so He can control our feelings. Satan wants to control our feelings so he can control
our minds." We must know the mind of Christ. The promises in scripture reveal His mind, His heart and His will.

There *is* power in God's word—not because of any "magic" or "secret formula" used during prayer in an attempt to manipulate God. We have a dependable Promissor Who stands behind His word. As we apply these scriptures in word and action, we empower God to move on our behalf or on the behalf of those we are praying for. If we don't share it, and continue to apply it to our life, we will lose everything we have gained. *You are My witnesses, says the Lord, and My servant whom I have chosen: that you may know and believe Me and understand that I am He.*—Isaiah 43:10. The equation is simple: **God first = fulfillment of God's destiny for our life**.

Jesus is coming soon. We cannot delay our preparation. My prayer is that this book has been life-changing for you; that its application will have become the breath of your soul and the determination of your heart.

If you faithfully apply all you have learned, you'll be ready to write your story for me to read. May God abundantly bless you as you grow in Jesus and become the sweet aroma of Christ. Prayer brings God's power into everything we do. There is no bad time to turn your life over to Jesus and secure a deeper heavenly rapport.

Remember:

"Those who exercise but little faith now, are in the greatest danger of falling under the power of satanic delusions and the decree to compel the conscience. And even if they endure the test they will be plunged into deeper distress and anguish in the time of trouble, because they have never made it a habit to trust in God. The lessons of faith which they have neglected they will be forced to learn under a terrible pressure of discouragement. We should now acquaint ourselves with God by proving His promises."[229]

For Your Assistance

If you need any further support, you can contact me on Facebook or through my website: **FreedomInSurrender.net**. I look forward to hearing from you and helping you in any way I can.

I pray you will be richly blessed and you will find hope and security in knowing God loves you; He loves you so much—"He can't take His eyes off of you." He longs to prove to you He is the God Who can be trusted.

"... nothing really happens regarding Christian growth until one prays and studies, that is, until one receives Christ. ... it is God's plan to change our lives into His likeness and as He does this, other people are attracted to Him; ... walk[ing] with the living, dynamic Christ."[230]

"We need to have far less confidence in what man can do and far more confidence in what God can do for every believing soul."[231]

"Your life is the sum of the responses you have made toward God. Once God makes Himself known to you, what you do next is your decision. Your reaction reflects what you believe about Him."
—Henry T Blackaby,
Experiencing God Devotional

Disclaimer

THOSE WHO KNOW ME are aware I have a home full of books and many, many file cabinets full of material. Some of this information I have filed and categorized since I was a very young child. As I became a teenager, if I saw an article or quotation I liked, I wrote it down as well. Sometimes, I just wrote down my own thoughts and filed them or put them on a 3 x 5 card and stuck them away. As I continued to grow and learn, I found when you keep material you need to record the sources as well. I hadn't done that with all the saved material.

I have many compilations of material I put together when I started speaking many years ago. I do not know for sure if all the references were cited there either. Some of these compilations I have used in this book.

To the best of my knowledge I have not included anyone else's work in my book unless I have given the reference or had permission to use it. If anything got past me, I humbly ask your forgiveness. My intention is to bring people to a deeper love and knowledge of our Savior, certainly not to claim someone else's work as my own. I hope this apology is for naught, but since I am such a hoarder of information, I felt it appropriate to waylay a potential problem by any oversight

I would also like to share my heart regarding the quotations I used in this book. Because I have quoted a particular author does not mean I endorse all they teach or believe. If they have made a profound statement that punctuates what I am teaching, then I have quoted them and credited their work. I like to look for the "good" in everyone and accentuate the positive.

"You can choose to be alert to the heart of God.
As you seek to understand what God is feeling, He
may share with you the intensity of His heart."
—Henry T Blackaby,
Experiencing God Devotional

Record of Experiences

This record of experiences will help you keep a list of the problems you had, the promises you claimed and the date your prayers were answered. It will help to increase your faith in the future when you can look back and see how God so miraculously intervened.

Date Asked	Problem	Promise Text	Date Answered	How Answered

"Prayer does not give you spiritual power. Prayer aligns your life with God so that He chooses to demonstrate His power through you"
—Henry T. Blackaby,
Experiencing God Day by Day

APPENDIX A: CONDITIONS TO ANSWERED PRAYER

According as His divine power hath given unto us all things that pertain unto life and godliness, through the knowledge of Him that hath called us to glory and virtue: Whereby are given unto us exceeding great and precious promises: that by these ye might be partakers of the divine nature, having escaped the corruption that is in the world through lust.
—2 Peter 1:3-4 KJV

2 Kings 19:1-20 KJV Obedience, acknowledgment of the Lord *... that which thou hast prayed to me ... I have heard.*

2 Kings 22:19 KJV Tender heart, humble, obedience, weeping *Because Thine heart was tender, and Thou hast humbled thyself before the Lord, when Thou heardest what I spake ... rent thy clothes and wept before me; I also have heard thee, saith the Lord.*

1 Chronicles 4:10 KJV Called on the Lord *And Jabez called on the God of Israel, saying, Oh that Thou wouldest bless me indeed, and enlarge my coast, and that Thine hand might be with me, and that Thou wouldest keep me from evil, that it may not grieve me! And God granted him that which he requested.*

2 Chronicles 6:37-42,7:12 KJV Repentance *And the Lord appeared ... and said unto him, I have heard thy prayer and have chosen this place to Myself for a house of sacrifice.*

2 Chronicles 7:14 KJV Humble yourself, pray, seek God, turn from evil ways *If My people, which are called by My name, shall humble themselves, and pray, and seek My face, and turn from their wicked ways; then will I hear from Heaven, and will forgive their sin, and will heal their land.*

2 Chronicles 30:27 Bless others *Then the priests the Levites arose and blessed the people: and their voice was heard, and their prayer came up to His holy dwelling place, even unto heaven.*

2 Chronicles 34:27 KJV Heart responsive, humbled before God, wept *Because thine heart was tender, and thou didst humble thyself before God, when thou heardest His words against this place, and against the inhabitants thereof, and humblest thyself before me, and dist rend thy clothes, and weep before me; I have even heard thee also, saith the Lord.*

Psalm 4:3 KJV Godly *But know that the Lord hath set apart him that is godly for Himself: the Lord will hear when I call unto Him.*

Psalm 18:6 KJV The distressed call and cry out *In my distress I called upon the Lord, and cried unto my God; He heard my voice out of His temple, and my cry came before Him, even into His ears.*

Psalm 37:4 KJV Delight in the Lord *Delight thyself also in the Lord; and He shall give thee the desires of thine heart.*

Psalm 40:1 KJV Patience *I waited patiently for the Lord and He inclined unto me, and heard my cry.*

Psalm 55:17 Faithfulness in praying and cry out loud *Evening, and morning, and at noon will I pray, and cry aloud: and He shall hear me.*

Proverbs 15:29 Righteous *The Lord is far from the wicked: but He heareth the prayer of the righteous.*

Isaiah 30:19 KJV Cry out to God *... thou shalt weep no more: He will be very gracious unto thee at the voice of thy cry; when He shall hear it, He will answer thee.*

Jeremiah 29:12-13 Seek for God with whole heart *Then shall ye call upon Me, and ye shall go and pray unto Me, and I will hearken unto you. And ye shall seek me, and find me when ye shall search for Me with all your heart.*

Daniel 10:12 KJV Desire to understand God, chasten self *Then said He unto me, Fear not, Daniel: for from the first day that thou didst set thine heart to understand, and to chasten thyself before thy God, thy words were heard, and I am come for thy words.*

Micah 7:7 KJV Wait *Therefore I will look unto the LORD; I will wait for the God of my salvation: my God will hear me.*

Matthew 6:12,14 KJV Forgiveness *And forgive us our debts, as we forgive our debtors. For if ye forgive men their trespasses, your heavenly Father will also forgive you:*

Matthew 6:33 KJV Seek first the kingdom of God *But seek ye first the kingdom of God, and His righteousness; and all these things shall be added unto you.*

Matthew 7:7 KJV Ask, seek, come to God *Ask, and it shall be given you; seek, and ye shall find; knock, and it shall be opened unto you.*

Matthew 8:13 KJV Believe for healing *And Jesus said unto the centurion, Go thy way; and as thou hast believed, so be it done unto thee. And his servant was healed in the selfsame hour.*

Matthew 18:19-20 KJV When two agree *Again I say unto you, That if two of you shall agree on earth as touching any thing that they shall ask, it shall be done for them of My Father which is in heaven. For where two or three are gathered together in My name, there am I in the midst of them.*

Matthew 21:22 KJV Ask and believe *And all things, whatsoever ye shall ask in prayer, believing, ye shall receive.*

Mark 2:17 KJV Feel our need of God *When Jesus heard it, He saith unto them, They that are whole have no need of the physician, but they that are sick: I came not to call the righteous, but sinners to repentance.*

Mark 11:25 KJV Forgiveness *And when ye stand praying, forgive, if ye have aught against any; that your Father also which is in heaven may forgive you your trespasses.*

Luke 8:50 KJV Believe for healing *But when Jesus heard it, He answered Him, saying, Fear not: believe only, and she shall be made whole.*

John 14:13-14, 15:16, 16:23 KJV Ask in Jesus' name *And whatsoever ye shall ask in My name, that will I do, that the Father may be glorified in the Son. If ye shall ask anything in My name, I will do it.*
Ye have not chosen Me, but I have chosen you, and ordained you, that ye should go and bring forth fruit, and that your fruit should remain; that whatsoever ye shall ask of the Father in my name, He may give it you.
Ye have not chosen me, but I have chosen you, and ordained you, that ye should go and bring forth fruit, and that your fruit should remain; that whatsoever ye shall ask of the Father in My name, He may give it you.

John 14:27 Let not heart be troubled or afraid *Peace I leave with you, My peace I give unto you: not as the world giveth, give I unto you. Let not your heart be troubled, neither let it be afraid.*

John 15:7 KJV Abide in Christ and words abide in us *If ye abide in me, and my words abide in you, ye shall ask what ye will, and it shall be done unto you.*

Acts 7:34 KJV Groaning *I have seen the affliction of My people which is in Egypt, and I have heard their groaning, and am come down to deliver them. And now come, I will send thee into Egypt.*

Acts 10:30-31 KJV Fasting ... *four days ago I was fasting ... and prayed ... thy prayer is heard ...*

Romans 12:2 KJV Be not conformed to world but transformed *And be not conformed to this world: but be ye transformed by the renewing of your mind, that ye may prove what is good, and acceptable and perfect will."*

Romans 15:13 KJV Believe *Now the God of hope fill you with all joy and peace in believing that ye may abound in hope, through the power of the Holy Ghost.*

Ephesians 6:18 KJV Pray in the Spirit, perseverance, intercede for others *Praying always with all prayer and supplication in the Spirit, and watching thereunto with all perseverance and supplication for all saints.*

Philippians 4:6 Pray with thanksgiving *Be careful for nothing; but in everything by prayer and supplication with thanksgiving let your requests be made known unto God.*

Colossians 4:2 KJV Continue in prayer with thanksgiving *Continue in prayer, and watch in the same with thanksgiving;*

Hebrews 3:14 KJV Hold confidence *For we are made partakers of Christ, if we hold the beginning of our confidence steadfast unto the end;*

Hebrews 6:12 KJV Faith, patience and no slothfulness *That ye be not slothful, but followers of them who through faith and patience inherit the promises.*

Hebrews 10:23 KJV Hold fast faith without wavering *Let us hold fast the profession of our faith without wavering; for He is faithful that promised.*

Hebrews 10:36 KJV Patience, do will of God *For ye have need of patience, that, after ye have done the will of God, ye might receive the promise.*

Hebrews 11:6 Faith, belief, diligence in seeking God *But without faith it is impossible to please Him: for he that cometh to God must believe that He is, and that He is a rewarder of them that diligently seek Him.*

Hebrews 12:15 KJV Diligence *Looking diligently lest any man fail of the grace of God; lest any root of bitterness springing up trouble you, and thereby many be defiled;*

1 John 1:9 Confession *If we confess our sins, He is faithful and just to forgive us our sins, and to cleanse us from all unrighteousness.*

1 John 3:21-22 KJV No heart condemnation, keep commandments and do right *Beloved, if our heart condemn us not then have we confidence toward God and whatsoever we ask, we receive of Him, because we keep His commandments, and do those things that are pleasing in His sight.*

1 John 5:14-15 KJV Ask according to God's will *And this is the confidence that we have in Him, that, if we ask any thing according to His will, He heareth us: and if we know that he hear us, whatsoever we ask, we know that we have the petition that we desired of Him.*

1 John 5:16 KJV Concern and intercession for others *If any man see his brother sin a sin which is not unto death, he shall ask, and he shall give him life for them that sin not unto death ...*

Jude 1:20 Pray in the Holy Spirit *But you, beloved, building yourselves up on your most holy faith, praying in the Holy Spirit,*

Revelation 3:20-21 KJV Hear God's voice and open heart to Him *Behold, I stand at the door, and knock: if any man hear My voice, and open the door, I will come in to Him, and will sup with Him, and He with Me. To him that overcometh will I grant to sit with Me in My throne, even as I also overcame, and am set down with My Father in His throne.*

"There has never been a time when the people of God have had greater need to claim His promises than now. Let the hand of faith pass through the darkness and grasp the arm of infinite power."
—Ellen G. White,
In Heavenly Places

Appendix B: Bible Promises

By getting acquainted with God through proving His promises in Jesus, we come to know God as our personal Friend and Savior. We learn the victory and hope won for us on the cross of Christ.

Promises for Forgiveness

Isaiah 43:25	He will not remember our sins
Jeremiah 31:34	Forgive iniquity and remember sin no more
Romans 8:1	No condemnation
1 John 1:9	If we confess, He will forgive

Promises for Christ Character and Spiritual Issues

Deuteronomy 5:32-33	Do what Lord has commanded, so you may live, prosper, and prolong your days
Joshua 1:3,9	Give you everywhere you put foot and be strong, courageous; do not be terrified or discouraged
Psalm 20:6	Saves His anointed with power.
Jeremiah 31:33	Write Law in our hearts
Jeremiah 32:27	God of all flesh can do anything
Jeremiah 32:38	You shall be My people
Ezekiel 36:26	A new heart and spirit

Luke 11:13	The infilling of the Holy Spirit
Luke 12:12	Holy Spirit teaches us what to say
Luke 24:45	Understand scripture
John 1:12	Receive Jesus, become sons of God
John 14:26	Holy Spirit, teach and bring to our remembrance
John 16:13	Holy Spirit will guide you to truth
Galatians 5:22-26	Fruit of Spirit
Ephesians 3:16	Inner man strengthened by Spirit
Ephesians 4:24	Put on new man
Philippians 2:5	Mind of Jesus
Colossians 3:15	Peace of God
1 Thessalonians 2:13	Words of truth will work in us
1 Thessalonians 3:13	Establish our heart in holiness
1 Thessalonians 5:24	He will help us do what He has called us to do
Hebrews 3:14	Partakers of Christ
Hebrews 10:19-22	Come boldly to throne of grace
2 Peter 1:4	Divine nature
1 John 3:2	Sons of God

Promises for Witnessing

Exodus 4:12	Teach us what to say
Job 33:3	Utter knowledge clearly
Isaiah 50:4	Have tongue of the learned, know what to speak
Isaiah 65:23	Labor not in vain
Jeremiah 1:7	He will send us
Jeremiah 1:9	God will put His words in our mouth

Promises Especially for Family

Genesis 2:18	Companion suited to our needs
Genesis 3:15	Enmity between our children and evil associates
Genesis 3:16	Desire to husband
Genesis 16:11	Lord heard misery and gave son
Genesis 17:20	As for Ishmael, I have heard thee, I will bless him—fruitful
Genesis 29:34	Leah not loved, God heard—gave son
Psalm 86:16	Save sons
Proverbs 1:8	Sons hear instruction
Proverbs 3:1	Sons forget not law

Isaiah 49:25	God will save our children
Hosea 2:19-20	Betrothed forever to spouse and God, in righteousness, loving-kindness, faithfulness.
Zephaniah 3:13	Not do iniquity, nor speak lies
Malachi 2:15	Have Godly children from union
Mark 10:8-9	The two become one
Luke 1:17	Turn hearts of fathers to children
Luke 2:40	Child grow in spirit, wisdom, and grace
John 17:21	Be one in Jesus
1 Corinthians 11:3	Head of man is Christ, head of woman is man
Ephesians 5:22	Wives submit to husbands
Ephesians 5:25	Husbands love wives
Ephesians 6:1	Children obey
Ephesians 6:4	Parents don't provoke children
Philippians 2:2-4	Likeminded, same love
Hebrews 13:1	Brotherly love
Hebrews 13:4	Marriage bed undefiled

Promises to Save from the Devil and Temptations

Ezekiel 44:23	Know difference between holy and profane
2 Kings 13:4	Lord listened to him for He saw how severely His people were being oppressed
Psalm 17:6-7	Those who take refuge in Him, He will save
Isaiah 33:15-16	Walk righteously and speak right, no contemplating evil, reject gain from extortion, no bribes or murder
Isaiah 54:17	No weapon formed against us will prosper
Luke 4:8	Satan behind us, worship Lord
John 8:36	Jesus will set you free from whatever binds you
John 10:27-28	Will not be taken from Jesus' hand
Acts 26:18	Turn from power of Satan
Romans 16:20	God of peace will bruise Satan
1 Corinthians 10:13	No temptation more than we are able to bear
2 Corinthians 7:1	Cleansing from filthiness of flesh and spirit

2 Corinthians 10:3-6	Casting down imaginations and everything that exalteth against the knowledge of God
Ephesians 6:11-19	Armor of God
Colossians 2:5	Triumph over Satan
James 4:7	Resist devil, he will flee

General Promises

Exodus 31:3	Fill with wisdom, knowledge, understanding
Exodus 5:13	Fulfill work, daily tasks
Deuteronomy 1:21	Fear not nor be discouraged
1 Kings 9:3	I have heard prayer and plea, I have consecrated temple which you built by putting My name there forever
Nehemiah 8:10	Joy of Lord is our strength
Psalm 19:3	Hears every speech and language
Psalm 19:13	Keep from presumptuous sins
Psalm 19:14	Words of mouth and meditation of heart acceptable
Psalm 28:8	Lord is our strength
Psalm 31:24	Courage
Psalm 32:8	God will instruct, teach and guide

Psalm 34:7	Angels will encamp round about
Psalm 34:13	Keep tongue from evil
Psalm 46:1	God is refuge and strength
Psalm 56:11	Trust in God, not man
Psalm 73:28	Put trust in God
Psalm 86:11	Learn God's ways
Psalm 103:3	Heal our diseases
Psalm 119:105	Word is our lamp
Psalm 138:8	Lord will perfect that which concerns us
Psalm 141:3	Set a watch, Lord, over our mouth
Isaiah 40:31	Strength renewed
Isaiah 41:17-18	Poor and needy search for water—I will answer them
Isaiah 49:8	In an acceptable time have I heard you, day of salvation, I have helped you
Isaiah 65:24	God will answer even before we call
Hosea 14:4	Heal backsliding
Jeremiah 33:3	Reveal secrets
Malachi 3:10	Windows of heaven opened

Matthew 9:29	According to our faith
Mark 5:34	Faith makes us whole
Luke 12:2	Reveal secrets
John 11:22	Ask and it will be given
Romans 8:28	All things work together for good
Romans 12:13	Given to hospitality
Romans 15:4	Through scriptures for learning and hope
1 Corinthians 3:9	Laborers with God
2 Corinthians 4:16	Inward man renewed
Galatians 1:10	Not men pleasers but servants of God
Ephesians 4:29	No corrupt communication
Ephesians 4:32	Kind, tenderhearted
Philippians 3:18-21	Appetite
Colossians 1:9-14	Filled with knowledge of God's will
2 Timothy 1:7	Not fear but love
Hebrews 12:15	No bitterness
James 1:5	Wisdom
James 5:15	Prayer of faith shall save sick
1 Peter 2:11	Abstain from fleshly lusts

1 Peter 3:8	Be of one mind, compassion
1 Peter 5:6	Humble self, God will exalt
1 Peter 5:7	Cast cares upon God
1 John 3:18	Love in deed and truth
1 John 4:18	No fear
Revelation 3:8	Keep word, open door to God
Revelation 3:18	Anoint eyes that we may see

Promises of Joy and Assurance

Nehemiah 8:10	Joy of the Lord our strength
John 14:13	I will not leave you comfortless
Romans 8:28	All things work together for good
John 15:11	My joy be in you
Psalm 34:3	Happy is man who takes refuge in Lord
Psalm 16:11	Show path of life fullness of joy
Psalm 32:1	Happy whose disobedience forgiven
Galatians 5:22,23	Fruits of the Spirit
Proverbs 3:5,6	Trust in Lord, make straight paths
Job 22:21	Acquaint self with Him and be at peace

Joshua 1:9	Be strong and of good courage
Luke 21:36	Pray for strength to escape
3 John 2	Enjoy good health
1 John 5:5	Overcome world through Jesus
Psalm 34:18	Lord close to brokenhearted
Jeremiah 29:11	Lord had good plans
Psalm 32:8	Make you wise; guide you and watch over
Isaiah 26:3	Perfect Peace

For additional promises for healing and ministering to the suffering, see Derry's books: **Heaven Touches Earth— Handbook for Supporting Sick, Terminally Ill and Dying** *and* **Heaven Touches Earth—Healing and Deliverance Scriptures and Prayers.**

Both books are available on Derry's website: **FreedomInSurrender.net** *or on* Amazon.com.

Appendix C: Spiritual Warfare Suggested Prayers

These prayers are only guidelines. Feel free to omit anything that does not apply to your situation and include anything that suits your prayer needs.

Embassy Prayer: A Prayer for Home Protection

By Winston Ferris of Blessing Tree Publications

We are not paranoiac when feeling concern about the insidious threats facing our homes and families today. How can we better protect our homes and loved ones from those subtle spiritual influences trying to demolish our marriages, family relationships, ministries and personal relationships to God? Wrestling with this problem, we find a solution/victory in the promise of 2 Corinthians 5:20, "Now then we are ambassadors for Christ ..." The words come alive with meaning. We are called to actively represent God in a society hostile to Him. That would make us **ambassadors**.

An **ambassador** lives and works in an embassy and that is what our home and work places are.

An embassy is not part of the country where it is located. It is literally territory of the country it represents. That means we can consider our homes as part of the Kingdom of heaven which we represent.

The ruler of the host country has no right to enter an embassy unless formally invited, God's enemy has no right to invade and influence our homes.

The full armed might of the kingdom we represent backs the inviolability of the embassy, for to violate the embassy is to literally insult and invade the country it represents. That means we can expect the armies of heaven to protect our homes.

Am embassy is traditionally a place of refuge for persecuted people to seek social asylum. Our homes can be a protected refuge for hurting citizens of the world seeking relief.

From these simple facts we can form a prayer of protection:

Heavenly Father, Lord of the Universe:

I come to You in the Name of the Lord Jesus Christ rejoicing. I rejoice for this new day which You have given me. I rejoice in the fact that I am Your child, a citizen of Your Kingdom, a member of Your personal family, a joint-heir with Jesus. I praise You for Your miracles of mercy to me, and reaffirm before You my desire to serve You, and only You, all the days of my life.

Your word tells me that You have chosen me to be an ambassador, one of Your accredited representatives on earth. I accept that responsibility, not because I am worthy—for I am not—but because You have given me the privilege. I lean on You, depend on You, for the wisdom and strength to represent You well in this world controlled by Your enemy.

Therefore, based on Your own Word, this day, as Your ambassador, I humbly present my home, work place, churches, and schools, as embassies of the Most High God. I affirm that they are not part of the kingdom of this earth, but literally part of the Kingdom of Heaven which I represent. I claim these embassies and the properties on which they stand to be sacred soil. Satan the usurping ruler of this world, has no legal right to enter these embassies or properties; nor do any of his representatives, supernatural or human.

Further Lord, I ask for a special contingency of Your holy angels to be sent to make safe these embassies. I ask for a shield-wall of angels to stand on the border of these properties, glory overlapping glory—surrounding them with an

*unbroken line, forming a barrier through which Satan can-
not come and within which he cannot function.*

*I reverently ask for a dome of spiritual glory to be raised
over our embassies, forming a shield of light protecting all
who live here or come within embassy precincts. I ask for a
security guard of angels to search these premises and identify any hidden presence of evil, to arrest that evil and expel
it.*

*If there are any areas of my life or the life of any of my fam-
ily members or occupants here which have consciously or
unconsciously given invitation to Satan or his representatives to establish their influence within the shield wall, I re-
pudiate those choices and reject their presence here. Accept, in Jesus' name, the sacrifice of my intention. Reveal
such areas to me and I will correct them, by Your grace.*

*Now, Lord Jesus, I invite You to fill these embassies with
Your presence. Let Your Holy Spirit flood these embassies
with His presence and fill our lives with His power, shedding the love of God abroad in our hearts. Let these embassies overflow with Your love and peace. Let angels love to
visit, finding a place of respite as they hurry to and fro in
earth's darkness laboring for men. Lord make our embassies a refuge for all who need sanctuary from this world.
Let my fellow children of God love to visit, feeling the at-
mosphere of heaven that heals and strengthens them in
their lives.*

*Let those under Satan's tyranny find freedom and release
from the fear, grief and suffering his service causes. Let
them be always welcome and let them sense the difference
in this place. And sensing the difference, lead them to question why, that we may tell them the wonderful story of Your
love. Let all who seek help, find it, and none be turned
away.*

*Finally Lord, I ask You for the gift of extending the embassy
blessing and protection to our own children and grandchil-
dren and to those whom You have given us, to our work-*

places, the schools where our children/grandchildren at-
tend, and any places You have in mind for us to go this
day. Some of our children are grown and gone from home,
yet they are still children of this home. Let embassy bless-
ing and protection surround them. Those spiritual children
and family You have given us—extend to them the bless-
ings of embassy security and healing also.

Father, again I rejoice in You. Make us worthy in Jesus to
be Your Ambassadors ... sensitive to human needs; com-
passionate toward all, even the unlovely, hypocritical, self-
righteous, repulsive and irritating. Give me wisdom to see
each need and deal with it in You—waiting patiently until
Your time to touch lives. Make me and my family, O Lord,
good ambassadors of Your Kingdom—That Your will may
be finished, and we behold the Holy City descend, and the
Kingdom of Heaven is joined with the recreated earth king-
dom, and all become one in Jesus. In His Name we ask it
and receive it done, with high praise.

AMEN

As this prayer has been prayed, subtle changes have
taken place within homes and families. Friends comment
on the restful feeling they experience while visiting. Life
takes on a calm and peace not previously enjoyed. Evidence indicates that this prayer, the Embassy Prayer, is
built on a sound, powerful prayer dynamic. Use it daily
and watch the results.

PRAYER OF COMMITMENT

Author Unknown

Heavenly Father,

I bow in worship and praise before You. I cover my family and myself with the blood of the Lord Jesus Christ as our protection during this time of prayer. I surrender myself completely and unreservedly in every area of my life to Yourself. I do take a stand against all the workings of Satan that would hinder me in this time of prayer, and I address myself only to the true and living God and refuse any involvement of Satan in my prayer.

Satan, I command you in the name of the Lord Jesus Christ, to leave my presence, to leave the presence of my spouse and our family members and the presence of all the people on our prayer lists, and acquaintances God has given us, with all of your demons. I bring the blood of the Lord Jesus Christ, our Savior, between us.

In the name of the Lord Jesus Christ, I come against every, generational curse, rash declaration, vows and judgments, every curse, every negative prayer, negative thought, look word or action; every hex, vex, chant, spell, voo-doo, white magic, black magic, and every demon named and unnamed assigned against my spouse, our families, me, and those I have mentioned. I reject, renounce and bind you. I break your power and I cancel your assignments and effects in Jesus' name. I cover my spouse, our families, me and all that I've mentioned and all that we have to do with the Blood of Jesus.

Father, I ask that You replace every evil and demonic with godly, positive traits, righteousness and health. I worship You, and I give You praise. I recognize that You are worthy to receive all glory and honor and praise. I renew my allegiance to You and pray that the Blessed Holy Spirit would enable me in this time of prayer. I am thankful, Heavenly Father, that You have loved us from past eternity, that You sent the Lord Jesus Christ into the world to die as our substitute that we would be redeemed. We are thankful that the Lord Jesus Christ came as our representative and that through Him You have completely forgiven us. You have given us eternal life. You have given us the perfect righteousness of the Lord Jesus Christ so we are now justified. We are thankful that in Him you have made us complete, and that You have offered Yourself to us to be our daily help and strength. I ask for a spiritual blood transfusion— fill us with the blood of Jesus to replace anything impure.

Heavenly Father, come and open our eyes that we might see how great You are and how complete Your provision is for this new day. We do, in the name of the Lord Jesus Christ, take our place with Christ in the heavenlies with all principalities and powers of darkness and wicked spirits under our feet. We are thankful that the victory the Lord Jesus Christ won for us on the cross and in His resurrection, has been given to us and that we are seated with the Lord Jesus Christ in the heavenlies; therefore, we declare that all principalities and powers and all wicked spirits are subject to us in the name of the Lord Jesus Christ.

We are thankful for the armor You have provided, and we put on the girdle of truth, the breastplate of righteousness, the sandals of peace, and the helmet of salvation. We lift up the shield of faith against all the fiery darts of the enemy, and take in our hand the sword of the Spirit, the Word of God, and use Your Word against all the forces of evil in our lives; and we put on this armor and live and pray in complete dependence upon You, Blessed Holy Spirit.

We are grateful, Heavenly Father, that the Lord Jesus Christ spoiled all principalities and powers and made a show of them openly and triumphed over them in Himself. We claim all that victory for our lives today. We reject out of our lives all the insinuations, the accusations, and the temptations of Satan. We affirm that the Word of God is true, and we choose to live today in the light of God's Word.

We choose, Heavenly Father, to live in obedience to You and in fellowship with Yourself. Open our eyes and show us the areas of our lives that would not please You. Work in our lives that there be no ground to give Satan a foothold against us. Show us any area of weakness. Show us any area of our lives that we must deal with so that we would please You. We do in every way today stand for You and the ministry of the Holy Spirit in our lives.

By faith, and in dependence upon You, we put off the old man and stand into all the victory of the crucifixion where the Lord Jesus Christ provided cleansing from the old nature. We put on the new man and stand in the victory of the resurrection and the provision He has made for us there, to live above sin. Therefore, in this day, we put off the old nature with its selfishness, and we put on the new nature with its love. We put off the old nature with its fear and we put on the new nature with its courage. We put off the old nature with its weakness and we put on the new nature with its strength. We put off today the old nature with all its deceitful lusts and we put on the new nature with all its righteousness and purity.

We do, in every way, stand into the victory of the ascension and the glorification of the Son of God where all principalities and powers were made subject to Him, and we claim our place in Christ, victorious with Him over all the enemies of our soul. Blessed Holy Spirit we pray that You would fill us. Come into our lives, tread down every idol and cast out every foe.

We are thankful, Heavenly Father, for the expression of Your will for our daily lives as You have shown us in Your Word. We therefore claim all the will of God for today. We are thankful that you have blessed us with all spiritual blessings in Heavenly places in Christ Jesus. We are thankful that You have made provision so that today we can live filled with the Spirit of God with love, joy and self-control in our lives. We recognize that this is Your will for us, and we therefore reject and resist all the endeavors of Satan and of his demons to rob us of the will of God. We refuse in this day to believe our feelings, and we hold up the shield of faith against all the accusations and against all the insinuations that Satan would put in our mind. We claim the fullness of the will of God for today.

We are thankful, Heavenly Father, that the weapons of our warfare are not carnal, but mighty through God to the pulling down of strongholds, to the casting down of imaginations and every high thing that exalts itself against the knowledge of God, and to bring every thought into obedience to the Lord Jesus Christ. Therefore, in our own lives today, we tear down the strongholds of Satan and we smash the plans of Satan that have been formed against us. We tear down the strongholds of Satan against our mind and we surrender our mind to You, Blessed Holy Spirit. We affirm Heavenly Father that you have not given us the spirit of fear, but of power and of love and of a sound mind. We break and smash the strongholds of Satan formed against our will today, and we give our will to You, and choose to make the right decisions of faith. We smash the strongholds of Satan formed against our body today, and we give our body to You, recognizing that we are your temple and we rejoice in Your mercy and Your goodness.

Heavenly Father, we pray that now through this day You would quicken us: show us the way that Satan is hindering and tempting and lying and counterfeiting and distorting the truth in our lives. Enable us to be aggressive in prayer. Enable us to be aggressive mentally and to think Your thoughts after You, and to give You Your rightful place in our lives.

Again, we now cover ourselves with the blood of the Lord Jesus Christ and pray that You, Blessed Holy Spirit, would bring all the work of the glorification, and all the work of Pentecost into our lives today. We surrender ourselves to You. We refuse to be discouraged. You are the God of all hope. You have proven Your power by Your victory over all Satanic forces active in our lives, and we reject these forces.

In the name of the Lord Jesus Christ, we submit our minds, and our dream activities only to the work of the Holy Spirit. We bind up all the powers of darkness and forbid them to work in our dream activities, or in any part of our subconscious while we sleep and while we are awake.

Father, we submit our lives to You, this day to do Your work and to do it eagerly. You can use us, cleanse us, purge us, heal us, anoint us, teach us, and financially bless us, for we are Your children. You can use us any way You want to.

We pray in the name of the Lord Jesus Christ with thanksgiving.

AMEN

BINDING AND LOOSING

Author Unknown

In the name of the Lord Jesus Christ, I bind _____ and all of our family members, extended family, friends acquaintances, and me body , mind, soul and spirit to the will and purposes of God for our life.

I bind our mind, will, reactions, responses and emotions to the truth of God's will and provisions. I bind us to the truth and to the blood of Jesus and to His healing power, protection, covering and cleansing of emotions and physical health. I bind our mind to the mind of Christ, that the very thoughts, feelings, and purposes of His heart would be within our thoughts. I bind our feet to the paths of righteousness so that our steps would be steady and sure. I bind us to the work of the cross with all of its mercy, grace, love, forgiveness, and dying to self. I bind us to the healing and balancing power of the Holy Spirit. I bind us to God's commands, to the desire for revival, commitment, obedience and to the path we have been ordained to walk in.

I loose all generational bondage thinking and associated strongholds, strongholds around self-deception and every wrong thought from us. I loose all effects and bondages from us that may have been caused by mistakes we have made whether accidental or intentional.

I loose every old, wrong, ungodly pattern of thinking, attitude, idea, denial, desire, belief, motivation, and every wrong mind/body agreement we have about wrong behaviors, wrong habits and wrong ideas about the future. I loose the hold of any foul spirit the strongholds of unforgiveness, fear, distrust, anger, and any other stronghold for any here being prayed for. And I ask that they be replaced with godly attributes opposite of those broken.

I loose the power and effects of wrong agreements not in alignment with God's will, from us. I loose deceptions and lies the enemy has told and lacerate the evil imaginations the enemy has set up from our mind, and I loose the effects and influences of any soulish agendas, soul ties we have with other people. I loose the confusion and blindness of the god of this world from our mind that has kept us from seeing the light and truth from the Word of God. I call forth every precious word of Scripture that has ever entered into our mind and heart, that it would rise up in power and truth within us giving us a desire for more knowledge and truth. Help us embrace that truth with full commitment and loyalty. I cast down arguments, theories, reasoning, proud and lofty things, any misconceptions, lies or pretensions, that set themselves up against the knowledge of God, or misrepresent Him or His desires for us and call forth the truth of God's word, way and will. Remove the scales from our eyes and unstop our ears that we might know Your truth.

In the name of Jesus, I loose the power and effects of any harsh or hard words (word curses) spoken to, about, against, or by us, and claim the cleansing blood of Jesus over every negative word. May the Holy Spirit teach us to talk well and wisely, avoiding useless conversations, speaking often of You. May our words always bring consolation to those in sorrow, guidance to those who are confused, light to the ignorant, hope to those who despair, comfort to those who are troubled, and good advice to those in need. Take our lips and make them Yours. Take possession of our mind and make it an instrument of Your goodness and a channel of your truth. May we prefer to talk to God rather than to men and may we always bring You closer to them and them closer to You. Since it is Your desire, Heavenly Father, that we be made whole, body, mind, soul and spirit, we ask You to bless us in the covenant name of Jehovah-Rophe, Your Healer, and cleanse us in our spirit from any defilements from past generations and broken-heartedness holding us close in Your loving arms. Please bless us with the cleansing of our blood, since life is in the blood of Jesus Christ our Lord through His sacrifice on the cross. Bless our health and wholeness in our autoimmune system, our bones and digestive systems, every organ, system and cell of our bodies. Bless and heal every part of our brain that it will function as God intended it to. Bless us with a release from stress, anxiety, worry from our adrenal gland by Peace.

Please bless us with cleansing in our soul from every generational soul wound and stronghold of what was not the Truth in Christ. In the name of Jesus, I crush, smash, and destroy generational bondages of any kind from mistakes made at any point between generations. I destroy them right here, right now. They will not bind and curse any more members of these families. I bind and loose these things in Jesus' name . He has given me the keys and the authority to do so; forgetting the pain of our past; and embracing abundance and freedom, love and joy, in the future—even greater than the past. I ask for the outpouring of God's mercy, grace and His will in all areas of our life, our families, our ministries and those around us. In Jesus' Name,

Amen

PRAYER OF CANCELLATION

By Winston Ferris of Blessing Tree Publications

Heavenly Father,

Lord this morning we bring before Your throne

_____ ,

and we specially ask You for the gift of release from all negative influences from the past. As You look over the generations past, we ask that any actions taken that give Satan special rights to

_____

be covered and cancelled with the new Covenant Jesus sealed for us on Calvary. If there has been any human or occult curse placed on this family line, which has not been canceled, we cancel it now with the New Covenant blood of Jesus. If through parents' choice or

_____ 's

life choices, grounds have been given granting God's enemy special influence in

_____ 's

life, we take back those grounds by choice and consecrate them to our Lord Jesus. All negative memories, behavior patterns, hidden programming of traumatic experiences which provide doorways for evil to enter or influence

_____ 's

life, we now consecrate wholly to God—physical, mental, emotional, spiritual, social, vocational, financial. We proclaim Jesus as Lord of

_____ 's

life and rejoice that the pathway of becoming like the Lord Jesus has begun and the journey will not end until

_____

shall be like Him when He comes.

In Jesus' Name,

Amen

BIBLIOGRAPHY

Andreasen, M. L. (1957) Prayer. Mountain View, CA: Pacific Press

Bonds, E. M. (1920). Purpose In Prayer. Grand Rapid, MI: Baker Book House.

Bonds, E. M. (1924). The Reality of Prayer. Grand Rapids, MI: Baker Book House.

Bonds, E. M. (1931). The Weapon of Prayer. Grand Rapids, MI: Baker Book House.

Bonds, E. M. (1972). Power Through Prayer. Grand Rapids, MI: Baker Book House.

Bonds, E. M. (1976). The Necessity of Prayer. Grand Rapids MI: Baker Book House.

Bonds, E. M. (1977). Prayer and Praying Men Grand Rapids, MI: Baker Book House.

Bonds, E. M. (1979). The Essentials of Prayer. Grand Rapids, MI: Baker Book House.

Bonds, E. M. (1979). The Possibilities of Prayer. Grand Rapids, MI: Baker Book House.

Bunch, T. (1946). Prevailing Prayer Washington, DC: Review and Herald.

Christenson, E. (1971). What Happens When Women Pray. Wheaton, IL: Tyndale House.

Christian, U. (1971). The Kneeling Christian. Grand Rapids, MI. Zondervan.

Coon, G. A. (1966), The ABC's of Bible Prayer. USA: A Dynamic Bible Living Publication.

Coon, G. A. (1958). Path to the Heart. USA: Review and Herald Pub.

Coon, G. A. (1971) Please Pray. USA: A Dynamic Bible Living Publication.

Coon, G. A. (1974). The Science of Prayer—Its ABC's. USA: A Dynamic Bible Living Publication.

Coon, G. A. (1968). A Study Guide—The Prayer of Reception. USA: A Dynamic Bible Living Publication.

Coon, G. A. (1968). Youth Prays ... God Answers. USA: A Dynamic Bible Living Publication.

Engelkemier, J. (1979) Whatever It Takes Praying. USA: Hart Research Center.

Hasel, G. Covenant in Blood. USA:

Lall, B. M. (1987). Prayer: Heaven's Unlimited Power at Our Disposal. Berrien Springs, MI: Geetanjali.

Laubach, F. C. Prayer—-The Mightiest Force in the World. USA: Fleming H. Revell Co.

Law, Robert Lee. (1970) The Positive Way. Collegedale, TN: Southern Pub.

Lockyer, H. (1959). All the Prayers of the Bible. Grand Rapids, MI: Zondervan.

Marshall, C. (1971). Adventures in Prayer. Old Tappan, NJ: Fleming H. Revell Co.

Maxwell, R. (1995). If My People Pray. Boise, ID: Pacific Press.

Moody, D. L. Prevailing Prayer. Chicago, IL: Moody Press.

Momeau, R. J. (1993). More Incredible Answers to Prayer. USA: Review and Herald Pub.

Murray, A. (1981). The Prayer Life. USA: Whitaker House.

Murray, A. (1981). Waiting On God. USA: Whitaker House.

Ogilvie, L. J. (1982). Conversation With God. USA: Harvest House.

Ogilvie, L. J. (1983). Praying With Power. Ventura, CA: Regal Books.

Ortlund, A. (1979). Discipling One Another. USA: Word.

Ortlund, R. (1975) Lord, Make My Life A Miracle! USA: Regal Books.

Richards, H.M.S. (1989). Practical Secrets of the Spiritual Life. USA: Hampton Hill.

Sanders, J. O. (1980). Enjoying Intimacy With God. USA: Moody Press.

Shewmake, C. J. (1995). When We Pray for Others. USA: Review and Herald Pub.

Shewmake, C. J. (1989) Practical Pointers to Personal Prayer. USA: Review and Herald.

Shuler, J. L. (1974). Help In Time of Need. Washington D. C.: Review and Herald Pub.

Smith, C. M. (1971). How to Talk to God When You Aren't Feeling Religious. NY, NY: Bantam Books.

Thomson, J. G. (1959). The Praying Christ. Grand Rapids, MI: Wm. B. Eerdmans Publishing Co.

Torrey, R. A. (1924). The Power of Prayer. USA: Fleming H. Revell Co.

Unknown Christian. (1971) The Kneeling Christian. USA: Zondervan.

Venden, M. L. (1988). The Answer Is Prayer. (Vol. Pacific Press Publishing Assoc.). USA.

White, E. G. (1941). Christ's Object Lessons. USA: Review and Herald.

White, E. G. (1962). Communion With God. Mountain View, CA: Pacific Press.

White, E. G. (1940) Desire of Ages USA. Review and Herald.

White, E. G. (1923). Education. USA: Southern Pub.

White, E. G. (1948). Gospel Workers. USA: Review and Herald.

White, E. G (1950). The Great Controversy. USA: Pacific Press.

White, E. G. (1967). In Heavenly Places. USA: Review and Herald

White, E. G. (1930). Messages to Young People. USA: Southern Pub

White, E. G. (1942). The Ministry of Healing. Mountain View, CA. Pacific Press.

White, E. G. (1952). My Life Today. USA: Review and Herald.

White, E. G. (1937). Prayer for the Sick. USA: Review and Herald.

White, E. G. (1943). Prophets and Kings. USA: Pacific Press.

White, E. G. (1908). Steps to Christ. USA: Review and Herald.

White, E. G. (1948). Testimonies. Vol. 1-5, USA: Pacific Press.

Whyte, A. (1928). Lord. Teach Us to Pray New York, New York: Doubleday, Doran, & Co., Inc.

Wyon, O. The School of Prayer. Philadelphia. PA: The Westminster Press.

ENDNOTES

Part One

Our Covenant-keeping God

[1] Isaiah 30:18 KJV

[2] Nehemiah 1:8-9 NIV

[3] Ezekiel 36:28 NIV

[4] Jeremiah 32:38-41 NIV

[5] Deuteronomy 28:1 NIV

[6] Exodus 20:13 KJV

[7] Deuteronomy 26:17-18 NIV

An Invitation

[8] Proverbs 8:17 KJV

[9] White, Desire of Ages, 22

[10] Numbers 23:19 NIV

[11] Joshua 23:14 NIV

Praying the Prayer of Faith

[12] White, Education, 126

[13] Ogilvie, God's Best for My Life, January 15

[14] White, Christ's Object Lessons, 143

Praying in the "YES" of God

[15] White, Evangelism, 695

[16] White, Education, 257

[17] White, Thoughts From Mount of Blessings, 142

Praying in Faith or Presumption

[18] White, Desire of Ages, 126

[19] White, Desire of Ages, 126

[20] Numbers 14:44; 15:30-31

[21] White, Steps to Christ, 96

Part Two

Introduction to Prayer

[22] Hebrews 4:16

[23] White, The Great Controversy, 525

[24] Matthew 7:7

Why Pray?

[25] Hebrews 4:16

[26] John 15:11

[27] Joshua 7:6

[28] White, Desire of Ages, 200

How to Pray

[29] 1 Thessalonians 5:17

30 Luke 22:41

31 John 11:41

32 Deuteronomy 9:25

33 2 Samuel 12:16

34 Psalm 34:15

35 Psalm 119:164

36 Hebrews 4:16

37 Matthew 6:7, 8

38 John 16:23, 15:16

39 Ephesians 2:18

40 2 Peter 1:4

How God Answers Prayer

41 Romans 8:26, 27

42 White, Steps to Christ, 96

Christ as Our Example

43 Luke 5:16 NASB

44 Matthew 6:33, 7:7

45 Mark 1:32, 35

46 White, 2 Testimonies, 202

47 Luke 6: 12, 13

Praying in the "YES" of God

[48] Luke 9:18, 20

[49] Mark 9:7

[50] Mark 9:29

[51] Matthew 6:9-13

[52] White, This Day With God, 263

[53] 2 Corinthians 1:20 ESV

[54] Blackaby, Experiencing God, 10

Prayer for the Holy Spirit

[55] Romans 8:26,27

[56] White, Desire of Ages, 672

[57] White, Desire of Ages, 306

[58] White, 6 Testimonies, 456

[59] Romans 8:26-28 ESV

[60] White, Desire of Ages, 436

[61] John 16:7-13

[62] John 14:26 KJV

[63] 1 Peter 3:8

[64] White, Messages to Young People, 30

[65] White, Desire of Ages, 672

[66] White, In Heavenly Places, 22

[67] Ogilvie, God's Best for our Life, February 18

[68] Ephesians 5:18

[69] White, Thoughts From Mount of Blessings, 20

[70] John 14:16 KJV

**Open the Doors of Heaven with
Praise, Adoration and Thanksgiving**

[71] Hebrews 13:15 KJV

[72] Blackaby, Experiencing God, 93

[73] 2 Chronicles 5:13,14 KJV

[74] Blackaby, Experiencing God, 93

[75] Lall, Heaven's Unlimited Power at Our Disposal, 45

[76] Romans 8:28 KJV

[77] Philippians 4:4-6

[78] Ephesians 5:20

[79] White, In Heavenly Places, 36

Temptation, Repentance, Confession and Restitution

[80] Luke 21:36

[81] White, My Life Today, 316

[82] Psalm 66:18

[83] 1 John 1:8,9

[84] Galatians 1:10

85 White, Steps to Christ, 38

86 Luke 19:8; Leviticus 5:16

87 White, Prophets and Kings, 668

88 Romans 3:23

89 White, Thoughts From Mount of Blessings, 84

90 1 John 1:9

91 White, In Heavenly Places,111

92 Ogilvie, God's Best for my Life, February 20

Part Three

Prayer of Faith/Prayer of Reception

93 White, Education, 257

94 White, Education, 253

95 White, The Great Controversy, 525

96 White, Christ's Object Lessons, 147

97 White, Christ's Object Lessons, 148

98 Ephesians 2:8 KJV

99 2 Peter 1:4 KJV

Overview of Conditions for Answered Prayer

100 Romans 8:32 NIV

101 White, Desire of Ages, 125

[102] White, Education, 253

Prayer of Faith: Verbal Conditions for Answered Prayer

[103] White, Education, 258

[104] John 15:7

[105] Psalm 37:4

[106] White, Education, 257

[107] Isaiah 58:9

[108] White, Thoughts From Mount of Blessings, 130

[109] Mark 9:23

[110] Blackaby, Experiencing God, 40

[111] Ephesians 5:20 KJV

[112] 1 Thessalonians 5:17,18 KJV

[113] Philippians 4:6 KJV

[114] Ephesians 3:20

[115] Deuteronomy 3:23-29

[116] 1 Kings 3:7-14

[117] Ogilvie, God's Best for My Life, January 8

[118] Blackaby, Experiencing God, January 9

[119] Blackaby, Experiencing God, January 10

[120] White, Education, 258

Prayer of Faith Condition: Feel Our Need

[121] Psalm 138:8

[122] Psalm 73:26

[123] Job 13:15

[124] Philippians 4:13

[125] Blackaby, Experiencing God, 40

[126] White, Thoughts From Mount of Blessings, 130

[127] Blackaby, Experiencing God, 38

[128] Matthew 6:33

[129] White, Steps to Christ, 44

[130] White, Christ's Object Lesson, 333

[131] White, Education, 126

[132] White, Thoughts From Mount of Blessings, 76

[133] Philippians 4:6-8 LB

Prayer of Faith Condition: Ask in Jesus' Name

[134] White, Christ's Object Lessons, 147

[135] White, Gospel Workers, 178

[136] White, Thoughts from Mount of Blessings, 84

[137] John 15:16

138 John 16:26,27 ESV

139 John 14:16

140 An Unknown Christian, The Kneeling Christian, 76

141 John 14:6 KJV

142 White, In Heavenly Places, 39

Prayer of Faith Conditions: Perseverance and Diligence

143 White, In Heavenly Places, 68

144 Law, The Positive Way, 19

145 1 Thessalonians 5:17

146 White, Steps to Christ, 97

147 White, In Heavenly Places, 24

148 White, Steps to Christ, 96

149 Numbers 23:19

150 Psalm 105:19 NIV

151 White, Steps to Christ, 97

152 White, Steps to Christ, 97

153 Matthew 18:19-20 KJV

154 White, Steps to Christ, 98

**Prayer of Faith Conditions:
Responsive Heart, Humility, Repentance**

155 White, In Heavenly Places, 23

[156] White, In Heavenly Places, 23

[157] Revelation 3:20 KJV

[158] Hebrews 3:8 NIV

[159] Matthew 11:28 NIV

[160] Psalm 34:8 KJV

[161] 2 Chronicles 7:14 KJV

[162] White, In Heavenly Places, 28

Prayer of Faith Conditions: Obedience, Faith and Patience

[163] Matthew 17:20 KJV

[164] Romans 12:3 KJV

[165] White, In Heavenly Places, 19

[166] Hasel, Covenant in Blood, 33

[167] 1 John 3:22 KJV

[168] Leviticus 26:27,32,33

[169] Blackaby, Experiencing God, 65

[170] White, Christ's Object Lessons, 143

[171] Blackaby, Experiencing God, 65

[172] White, Desire of Ages, 24

[173] Ogilvie, God's Best for My Life, February 5

[174] Hebrews 11:8 KJV

175 Hasel, Covenant in Blood, 29

176 Galatians 3:7,9 NIV

177 Hasel, Covenant in Blood, 31

178 Ogilvie, God's Best for My Life, February 23

179 White, Steps to Christ, 96

180 Ogilvie, God's Best for My Life, February 28

181 White, In Heavenly Places, 71

Prayer of Faith Conditions: Love and Forgiveness

182 Acts 26:18 KJV

183 Colossians 3:14 KJV

184 John 15:12

185 John 8:11

186 Andreasen, Prayer, 98

187 1 John 1:9

188 Matthew 5:23,24

189 Psalm 79:9 KJV

190 Ephesians 4:26

191 Mathew 6:14, 15 KJV

192 Wyon, The School of Prayer, 148

193 Ephesians 4:29-32 KJV

[194] White, Thoughts From Mount of Blessings, 27

[195] Mark 11:25-26

[196] Ephesians 4:32 KJV

[197] Philippians 2:2-5 KJV

[198] Psalm 19:14 KJV

[199] Galatians 2:20

[200] Isaiah 55:7

[201] Blackaby, Experiencing God, 86

Intercession

[202] Psalm 103:12

[203] Isaiah 1:18

[204] White, Christ's Object Lessons, 197

[205] Isaiah 43:10,21

[206] Isaiah 43:7 KJV

[207] Luke 23:34

[208] Wyon, The School of Prayer, 150

[209] Exodus 32:31,32 NASB

[210] White, Steps to Christ 44-5

[211] White, Messages to Young People, 158

Part Four

Prayer of Commitment

[212] 1 Peter 2:24

[213] Matthew 8:17

[214] White, The Faith I Live By, 134

[215] Isaiah 57:1,2

[216] Luke 22:42 KJV

Spiritual Warfare

[217] Colossians 2:10,15 KJV

[218] Ephesians 6:12

[219] Ephesians 6:17

[220] White, In Heavenly Places, 253

[221] Romans 16:20 KJV

[222] White, 2 Testimonies, 509

Part Five

Hindrances to Answered Prayer: Cherished Sin

[223] Psalm 66:18 KJV

[224] Ezekiel 36:26,27 KJV

[225] 1 John 1:8

[226] 1 John 1:9

[227] Proverbs 28:9

[228] White, Desire of Ages, 141-2

Final Thoughts

[229] White, The Great Controversy, 622

For Your Assistance

[230] Zackrison, The Positive Way, Robert Lee Law, Foreword

[231] White, Christ's Object Lessons, 146

Other Titles by Dr. Derry James-Tannariello

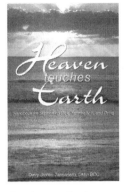

Heaven Touches Earth—Handbook for Supporting Sick, Terminally Il and Dying was *written to provide you with the skills and tools necessary to bring solace and comfort to the sick and suffering at home, in the hospital or hospice ministry.*

This concise "how-to handbook" is a succinct resource of clear insight into hospital practices and protocols useful in training volunteers, parish vistors, pastors and chaplains and a helpful refresher guide for those who have studied hospital ministry.

Also available in eBook format at Amazon.com or at **FreedomInSurrender.net**.

*This Scripture Travel Companion to **Heaven Touches Earth—Handbook for Supporting Sick, Terminally Il and Dying**, is a take-along resource containing only the Healing and Deliverance Scriptures and Prayers chapter of the Heaven Touches Earth book. It is designed for those ministering in a supportive role. (63 pages.)*

Also available in eBook format at Amazon.com or at **FreedomInSurrender.net**.

For gift or bulk orders of these, or any of Derry's books, please visit: **FreedomInSurrender.net**

UPCOMING TITLES

Look for the companion volume to
Living Volume One: Praying in the "YES" of God.

Living Volume Two:
Growing in the "YES" of God

God Has a Plan for Your Life! Do you wonder why it seems some people have answers to their prayers and unexplainable miracles in their life—and you don't? Is there really any such thing as security and joy? What does love mean? What if you could find the answers to these questions and more? You can.

This in-depth Bible Study on principles of a more effective prayer life, further growth in Jesus and living out His character and plans for your life victoriously and blessed will reassure you of God's love. It is best understood and most effective if preceded by **Living Volume One: Praying in the "YES" of God**.

With Gladness Every Day
and
With Kisses from Heaven

A multi-volume compilation of stories from a life lived in service, obedience and total dependence on God and His Mercy—Available 2017.

A compilation of stories of Answers to Prayer and Lessons from Scripture and Life Experiences from a life lived in service, obedience and total dependence on God and His Mercy

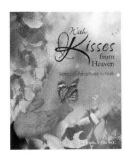

A compilation of stories with Spiritual Application and of God's Intervention from a life lived in surrender, faith, love and total dependence on God and His plans.

Why Not
Bless Others!!!

FreedomInSurrender.net

- ✓ Mention this book on your social media platforms; use the hashtag #PrayingInTheYesOfGod

- ✓ Are you a blogger? Consider writing a book review on your blog. Post it to your blog and other retail book outlets

- ✓ Know someone else who would be blessed by this book? Pick up a copy for a friend or coworker

- ✓ Recommend this book to your church library or small group study

- ✓ Share this message on Facebook. "I was blessed by *Praying in the "YES" of God* by Derry James-Tannariello and Freedom In Surrender Ministries

- ✓ Follow us on Facebook. Let us know what you like and stay up-to-date on upcoming new releases and pearls of wisdom from Derry!

 Facebook.com/FreedomInSurrenderMinistries
@FreedomInSurrender

 @PrayWithDerry

 /PrayWithDerry